# Homelessness: what can be done

## An immediate programme of self-help and mutual aid

### Ron Bailey

Jon Carpenter
Oxford

First published in 1994 by
Jon Carpenter Publishing,
PO Box 129, Oxford OX1 4PH.

ISBN 1 897766 09 2

Printed and bound by Biddles Ltd., Guildford and King's Lynn, England

# Dedication

This book is dedicated to the late Councillor Herbert Eames, Conservative Chair of the Housing Committee, London Borough of Lewisham, 1968-71, in admiration of the astonishing courage and vision he showed by entering into the first legal agreement with squatters in 1969.

As a result of his action, tens of thousands of homes that would otherwise have stayed empty have been brought back into use and hundreds of thousands of homeless people given new hope and dignity.

Ron Bailey
January 1994

| | |
|---|---|
| Written by: | **Ron Bailey** |
| Research: | **Melody Lovelace** |
| Research Assistance: | **Beren Money** |
| | **Paul Gaytan** |
| Editing and layout: | **Melody Lovelace** |
| Cover Design: | **Cherry Puddicombe** |

**Policy Pathways** is a series in which the Green Party explores and explains, in detail, exactly how it will implement its policies and what they will mean for this country.

**Homelessness - what can be done** is the fourth in the series. The first, which explained the Party's costed transport strategy, was entitled **Road to the Future** (price £5). The ideas in that document were further developed in **Traffic-Free Towns** (price £2). **Recession: the Way Out** (price £5) explained the Green Party's view of the current recession and offered a Green way out.

All these can be obtained from:
The Green Party, 10 Station Parade, Balham High Road, London SW12 9AZ (tel: 081-673 0045)

# Contents

# Glossary

**housing association** - a voluntary body set up to provide housing

**housing co-operative** - a housing association run on co-operative lines which provides accommodation for its own members

**Housing Corporation** - government-established statutory body that finances and oversees the activities of housing associations

**non-registered housing association** - a housing association that is not registered with the Housing Corporation; they are usually registered with the Registrar of Friendly Societies under the Industrial and Provident Societies Act 1965 and are usually the smaller, more community-based associations

**registered housing association** - a housing association registered with the Housing Corporation; they are usually the larger more 'official' associations

**secondary housing association** - a housing association that does not itself provide housing but whose role is to advise, enable, support or promote other housing associations to do so

**short-life accommodation** - accommodation provided for a short or temporary period only before the property is demolished; renovation works start; it is let permanently; or sold off

**short-life property** - property providing short-life accommodation as above

**statutory body** or **statutory organisation** - a body or organisation set up by Act of Parliament and given certain functions by that or other Acts

**voluntary body** or **voluntary organisation** - a non-statutory body or organisation run for socially beneficial purposes and not for profit

# 1 Homelessness

Homelessness means being without a home. Homeless people, unlike other members of our society, have either no accommodation or no permanent or settled accommodation—nowhere to call home.

People who sleep rough in the cardboard cities that have become an all-too-common feature of many of our urban centres are homeless.

Families placed in bed and breakfast, hostels or other short-stay accommodation by local authorities are homeless.

Those people who have nowhere to live but are turned away by local authorities simply because they do not fit into the correct legal categories for statutory housing are homeless. These include the people classed as 'intentionally homeless' and those *not* in the so-called priority classes for which councils have a legal responsibility.

The tens, if not hundreds, of thousands of people with nowhere to live who do not even bother to approach local authorities because they know there is no hope of any help are homeless. These include most single people and childless couples.

Those people forced to drift from friend to friend, relation to relation, sleeping on floors and in spare beds are homeless.

People whose only shelter is a squat or other place in which they have no lawful right to stay are homeless.

Those people (usually women) forced to leave otherwise secure homes for fear of violence are also homeless.

This book is about them. It is about them because it deals with homelessness and the policies that we believe are needed *forthwith* to deal with the problem.

Homelessness first sprang to the nation's attention in the

mid-sixties when certain events highlighted the plight of homeless people: at West Malling in Kent there was a year-long struggle to improve conditions at a hostel for homeless families; the public was deeply shocked when the television play *Cathy Come Home* was shown on BBC television; and a new charity came into being, Shelter, the National Campaign for the Homeless. Perhaps under-standably, Shelter concentrated on the plight of homeless families and so another organisation was formed to champion the cause of the single homeless and those without children. This was CHAR (the Campaign for the Homeless and Rootless). Since then, many more organisations have been formed and much excellent campaigning and provision of accommodation has come from these voluntary bodies. Also, in 1968, the current squatting movement began in East London; squatting is now the only hope of any sort of accommodation for tens of thousands of homeless people.

Yet the problem remains. There are nearly 150,000 people officially classed as homeless in the priority classes[1]; these are mainly homeless families. Recently, the Young Homelessness Group estimated that in one year 156,000 young people between the ages of sixteen and twenty-five slept rough—on the streets, in railway sidings, squats, derelict buildings, on floors and the like.[2] A recent report by Age Concern estimated that there are around 2,000 people over the age of fifty living on the streets and in hostels in London alone.[3]

Although the problem of homeless families is much worse in London than anywhere else, a recent report by CHAR stated that 'outside London there are more people sleeping rough and staying in temporary hostels.'[4] The report makes the point that, in 1991, there were 22,383 single homeless hostel places in London compared with only 37,759 in the rest of the country[5] and 11,694 single homeless claimants living in board and lodgings in London compared with 64,855 in the rest of the country.[6]

The problem now affects young people who are discharged from local authority care at the age of sixteen or seventeen. A recent study showed that 'social services departments are, in the main, failing to fulfill their responsibilities to homeless 16- and 17- year olds under the Children Act' and concluded that 'young people mainly remain homeless due to a shortage of appropriate, affordable, decent housing and a lack of appropriate support.'[7]

The official figures are the tip of the iceberg. There are also 40,000 squatters who have no lawful home; there are tens of thousands of single homeless and childless couples who are never included in the figures because they never approach any official bodies. The true extent of the problem is unknown, but it is certainly far greater than official statistics show.

The problem is widespread, affecting all sections of our society. Yet, local authorities only have a duty to provide accommodation for homeless people if they fall into a special category: that is, if they are in 'priority need'.[8] This category only includes families with dependent children, pregnant women, those who become homeless because of an emergency such as fire or flood and those who are vulnerable because of old age, illness, disability or other special reasons. In such cases, councils have a duty to provide both temporary and permanent housing, unless they decide that the person has become homeless intentionally because 'they have deliberately done or failed to do something that results in loss of accommodation.'[9] In such cases, there is only a duty to provide temporary accommodation for a sufficient time to allow the homeless person to find somewhere else to live.[10]

All homeless people not falling into those categories— most single people and childless couples—are not deemed to be in the priority classes and have no right to accommodation. The result is that little or no provision exists for these people.

The aim of this book is to explain Green Party policies and to show how all of this should be changed and how accommodation could be provided for all homeless people in the immediate and short term.

**Footnotes**

1. Department of the Environment figures
2. *If Youth Matters*, Young Homeless Group
3. *Older People in London*, Age Concern
4. *Counted Out* (p.5), Geoffrey Randall, CHAR/Crisis
5. ibid./DoE
6. ibid./DSS
7. *Reassessing Priorities* p.2, Jacqui McCluskey, CHAR
8. Housing Act 1985, Section 59
9. *In on the Act* p.43, Geoffrey Randall and Martin Todd, CHAR; see also Housing Act 1985, Section 60
10. ibid.; see also Housing Act 1985, Section 65

# 2 The issue of empty property

Empty property is not a new problem. Since homelessness became a national issue in the mid-sixties, there have been many exposés of long-term empty houses—usually those owned by local authorities and other public bodies—and numerous initiatives to ensure maximum use of empty property. One of these was started in 1975, when Shelter, with other charitable bodies, supported an idea by the author of this book and set up the Housing Emergency Office (later called the Empty Property Unit). The Housing Emergency Office was a national campaigning and enabling organisation whose sole aim was to bring empty houses into use. One of its most successful initiatives was to provide advice and model rules for a large number of self-help groups of homeless people, particularly single people. The official status of the groups was one of the factors that persuaded official bodies to hand over thousands of houses to them that would otherwise have stood empty.

Perhaps the biggest initiative of all came in January 1992 with the establishment of the Empty Homes Agency. This organisation is the brain-child of Antony Fletcher, long-time campaigner for the use of empty homes and currently the Special Adviser on Empty Property to the Housing Minister. The Empty Homes Agency was launched not only by Fletcher but also by Housing Minister, Sir George Young, Cardinal Basil Hume and a host of other eminent people. Headed by Bob Lawrence, a former housing officer and a man of infectious energy and enthusiasm, its declared task was to bring 20,000 empty properties into use.

However, despite very considerable successes, like all efforts over the last 25 years it has not succeeded in eradicating

5

# HOMELESSNESS - WHAT CAN BE DONE

the problem. Indeed, even the Adam Smith Institute has felt concerned enough about empty property to publish a new document with radical suggestions for solutions[1]—yet the wastage of property continues.

Recently, concern has focussed not only on empty publicly-owned houses but also on empty privately-owned homes, for here, too, the waste of resources has become only too apparent. Let us examine the statistical and anecdotal evidence concerning all types of empty and wasted homes.

## Local Authority-Owned Empty Homes

Table 1 shows the number and condition of vacant dwellings owned by local authorities over the past three years. Table 2 shows how many London council homes have been empty for more than six months and more than twelve months. We have included three years' figures in both these Tables to show that this waste of homes is not a one-off phenomenon.

**Table 1  Number and condition of void council dwellings**

|  | 1991 | 1992 | 1993 |
| --- | --- | --- | --- |
| Dwellings available for letting | 19,300 | 17,500 | 17,500 |
| Dwellings to be let after minor repairs | 24,100 | 22,900 | 22,300 |
| Dwellings undergoing major works | 10,700 | 9,400 | 9,100 |
| Dwellings awaiting major works | 9,700 | 6,500 | 5,200 |
| Dwellings to be sold | 8,000 | 5,200 | 6,600 |
| Dwellings awaiting demolition | 5,600 | 7,300 | 5,900 |
| Undesignated | 5,800 | 5,600 | 4,300 |
| **Total** | **83,200** | **74,500** | **70,900** |

Source: DoE National HIP Reports July 1991/1992/1993

**Table 2  London council homes empty for over 6 and 12 months (as at April 1st)**

|  | 1990 | 1991 | 1992 |
|---|---|---|---|
| Empty over 6 months | 9,028 | 8,334 | 6,798 |
| Empty over 12 months | 6,623 | 5,531 | 4,469 |

Source: 'Housing Needs and Resources', compiled by London Research Centre from L.A. HIP Returns

On the basis of past experience and tried-and-tested schemes alone (that is, even without any new initiatives) many of these empty homes could have been used to house families who are in bed and breakfast or single people sleeping on relatives' floors or in cardboard cities. Yet, they have remained empty.

The statistics raise two more important questions: How many of these homes have been empty for 2, 3, 5, or even 10 years? And how long are they likely to remain empty? Published evidence shows that some local authority-owned homes have been left empty for extraordinary lengths of time[2] and, although it is anecdotal, the evidence has been consistent enough to reveal that there is a very severe and persistent problem.

Let us look at a few examples:

• Take, for instance, Nos. 94 and 96 King George Street, London SE10. They were originally owned by the Inner London Education Authority and after its demise were passed to Greenwich Borough Council. No. 94 King George Street has stood empty for 30 years and No. 96 for a 'mere' 19 years.

• Consider, too, the case of Tower House, owned by the London Borough of Tower Hamlets, in Fieldgate Street, Stepney. A poster produced by The Empty Homes Agency best describes the situation: 'This 400 bedroomed hostel sits empty in its 5th year of idleness. This building was sought by a number of housing associations as a possible hostel. Political leaders from Stepney Neighbourhood feel its use as a hostel would "stigmatise" the area...the Council has turned down all offers of financial help from associations and even the Lord Mayors Appeal.' The EHA poster also points out that 'walking the few hundred yards from Aldgate East Station to Tower House, 43 rough sleepers were counted in August 1992' and adds, for historical interest, that 'the building was not boarded up in the 1920's, so George Orwell was able to stay in Tower House, refering to it in *Down and Out in London and Paris*.'[3]

Outside London there are numerous cases of council-owned properties being left to rot. The following examples are just two of many:

• Nos.144-156 York Road, Bedminster are owned by Bristol City Council; they are listed as being of special architectural and historical importance but they have been left empty for up to 25 years and are now just derelict shells.

• Nos. 24-32 (consecutive) Wilson Street, Bristol 8 have been left empty for between 16 and 23 years.

In his book *Homes Wasted*, Antony Fletcher reported that 'over the years several attempts were made by established local groups to get short-life use of the houses, but all these requests were refused' because of future plans 'about to take place'.[4] That was in 1982. In 1993, they are still empty and we can only agree with the leading member of Bristol City Council who is quoted by Fletcher as saying that the history of these properties is 'a bloody disgrace'.

These examples are gross by any standards. We have not even bothered to seek an official explanation for them: there are no explanations which could convince us that leaving homes to rot for up to 30 years is a reasonable policy.

The same is true in many other areas: houses abandoned and forgotten for years. Although the number of such homes may be statistically small they still represent a waste of resources, an insult to the homeless and a scandalous bungling of public policy that must end.

## Government-Owned Empty Homes

Government is keen to condemn local authorities for keeping houses vacant but the facts tell us that their own record is far worse. Of all public bodies, government departments leave the highest percentage of their housing stock empty, as Table 3 shows.

**Table 3  Vacant Homes**

|  | Total Vacant | % of Stock |
|---|---|---|
| Local Authorities | 75,000 | 1.9 |
| Housing Associations | 16,000 | 2.5 |
| Ministry of Defence | 10,500 | 15.0 |
| Other government departments | 5,000 | 13.0 |

Source: Empty Homes Agency booklet, 1993, quoting Department of the Environment sources

Consider, what the Empty Homes Agency has called, 'the street of shame'[5]: 48 flats in Shillingford Street, Westminster, left empty by the Ministry of Defence for five years. As long ago as January 1992, the Agency, 'made a rental offer to the MoD for a lease of the building. The Agency also offered to undertake pre-letting repairs, maintenance, contribute to outgoings and guarantee vacant possession at the end of the term. The MoD refused to negotiate.'[6] However, 'on 3rd February the MoD's contractors smashed windows and then stripped the buildings of plumbing fittings, radiators, sinks and other fixtures.'[7] The MoD claimed that the buildings were to be refurbished and 'when challenged by The Times six months later on progress, the MoD said that works were nearing completion and families would be moving in. Yet in May 1993 (i.e. one year later) the buildings sit untouched: exactly as MoD contractors had left them a year earlier.'[8]

There is a similar deception regarding 73 surplus homes at Biggin Hill in Kent, many of which have stood empty for some years.[9] Clive Soley MP continually urged the Minister to allow the properties to be handed over to a local housing association for use as social housing and eventually he was successful. However, on 19th May 1993, Mr Archie Hamilton MP told Mr Soley that 'a one-year lease on the 73 surplus properties was offered to housing associations but was not taken up.'[10] Thus, it is not the government's fault that these properties are still standing empty in December 1993: they did their best but the housing associations were just not interested. Sounds convincing—until you know the full story. What Mr Hamilton's Parliamentary reply does not reveal is that the housing association which was most interested would have taken over the houses for short-life use for homeless people but the government made it impossible for them to do so. The government made it a condition of any arrangement that the housing association must buy the houses at the end of the period—with money that they did not have. As the association's director told the Empty Homes Agency: 'It's like asking British Rail for a day return to Clacton only to discover you have to buy the train as well.'[11] Needless to say, the 73 houses still stand empty.

The extent of neglect and waste by the Ministry of Defence was revealed in Parliament on 11th January 1993 when the Minister admitted that 12.7% of service married quarters and 20.7% of civilian houses were empty.[12] More details were revealed in March 1993 when another Parliamentary Question elicited the reply that, on 31st December 1992, there were 9,253 vacant Ministry of Defence properties plus another 1,872 vacant surplus married quarters.[13]

There is more published information on empty houses owned by other government departments. The Department of Transport owns 3,432 houses which it has acquired in connection with road proposals: 721, or 21%, have been left empty.[14] The Department of the Environment has 18.3% of its homes empty;[15] the Department of Employment has 62% empty;[16] the Department of Social Security has 16.7% empty;[17] the National Heritage Department has 66% empty;[18] the Welsh department has 7.9% empty;[19] and finally, the Department of

Health had 14,000 units empty—15% of its total stock.[20]

Overall, government departments (excluding the Ministry of Defence) have 13% of their stock empty.[21]

Yet where are the shouts and clamours for action by Conservative M.P.'s who condemn local authorities for keeping houses empty?

## Privately-Owned Empty Homes

Official statistics show that publicly-owned empty property is just the tip of the iceberg: empty privately-owned houses are an even greater waste of resources, as Table 4 shows.

### Table 4  Vacant Private Sector Homes

| Total vacant | % of stock |
|---|---|
| 700,000 | 4.6 |

Source: DoE compilations from HIP Figures

These figures do not indicate the real extent of the problem. It is normal for houses to be empty for a month or two between occupants but there are many privately-owned houses which lie abandoned for years. We comment in Chapter 4 (Policy Initiative 2) on the need for more information about these houses. Here, as with publicly-owned homes, we give some evidence to demonstrate the nature of the problem.

• There are, for example, 400 empty flats in Artillery Row, London W1, just a quarter of a mile from Victoria Station. They could have provided decent accommodation for hundreds of families in bed and breakfast and single homeless people. These flats have been vacant for 10 years. All offers to use them, even by the Empty Homes Agency, have been refused.

• There is also the case of Munster Square vicarage in Camden, another area which has a desperate homelessness problem. The poster printed by the Empty Homes Agency

11

aptly sums up this scandal: 'This 12-bedroomed house was
occupied by students. The owner asked them to leave in order
to refurbish the house. The house stood empty. It was squatted.
The owner evicted the squatters. The house stood empty. It
was squatted. The owner evicted the squatters. The house still
stands empty—for at least six years.' The house is owned by
The London Diocese of the Church of England.

Empty houses are, therefore, a problem. In Chapter 4, we
make proposals to ensure that they can be brought back into
use to house the homeless, but first we tackle the issue of
politics and homelessness.

**Footnotes**

1. *Into the Voids*, Hartley Booth MP, Adam Smith Institute,
1993
2. For example: *Homes Wasted*, Antony Fletcher, Shelter, 1982;
*The Homeless and the Empty Houses*, Ron Bailey, Penguin, 1977
3. Empty Homes Agency Poster, 1993
4. Homes Wasted op.cit.
5. Empty Homes Agency Booklet, 1993
6. ibid.
7. ibid.
8. ibid.
9. Hansard, 11.5.93, cols. 457-458
10. Hansard, 20.5.93, col. 253
11. Empty Homes Agency Poster 1993
12. Hansard, 11.1.93, cols. 633-634
13. Hansard, 24.3.93, cols. 608-611
14. Hansard, 23.3.93, cols. 534-535
15. Hansard, 18.1.93, cols. 128-129
16. Hansard, 11.1.93, cols. 633-634
17. Hansard, 11.1.93, col. 678
18. Hansard, 13.1.93, col. 735
19. Hansard, 11.1.93, col. 668
20. Hansard, 11.1.93, col. 615

# 3 Politics and homelessness: Green Party principles

There are three principles underlying all Green Party policies: social justice; concern for the environment; and citizen involvement. We believe that the application of these principles to the homelessness problem in this country can lead to very constructive policies.

## 1. Social Justice

Let us begin by considering the most obviously relevant principle: social justice. Social justice means decent and fair treatment for all our citizens. It is indefensible, therefore, that families are left to rot in bed and breakfast establishments. It is indefensible that homeless single people are forced to live in cardboard cities. It is indefensible that childless couples have little prospect of decent housing in which to begin their lives together. It is indefensible that young people are discharged from care at the age of sixteen or seventeen only to become homeless. It is indefensible that people are discharged from mental hospitals to end up on the streets. Homelessness cannot be tolerated. This is the view of the Green Party.

Social justice in action means that every possible effort is made to solve the problem now, or at the very least, alleviate it. The guiding principle of any policy must be the interests of the homeless, not political dogma. If such a policy will improve life for homeless people—now—the intended action should be taken.

We have described the extent of the problem of homelessness. The current government's housing policy is a major cause but, even with massive government action, a

13

lasting solution to homelessness is, at best, a medium-term objective. We believe, therefore, that every possible action must be taken to provide as much short-term relief as possible. The homeless at present in bed and breakfast or cardboard cities and those likely to end up there in the next year or two, gain no comfort from knowing that things might improve in a few years time. For them, and all other homeless people, policy is only meaningful if it can improve their situations now.

The Green Party believes that the provision of emergency accommodation in short-life houses for homeless people is a justifiable policy for the immediate term, even if the accommodation itself is not perfect. The test must be: 'Is it better accommodation than the homeless would otherwise have had?' Emergency housing in a three-roomed, short-life house could be judged unsatisfactory for a family with three children but it is a lot better for that family than a year cooped up in one room in a bed and breakfast establishment, often miles away from their own area, and where they may have to vacate the premises during the day. In such a situation, social justice and the needs of the homeless dictate that every effort must be made to provide the (perhaps) unsatisfactory but preferable accommodation. It is not helpful for politicians or anyone else to argue that these families should not be housed in such accommodation because 'substandard accommodation should not be provided even for homeless people'. Such a 'pure' policy condemns the very same homeless families to years in seedy bed and breakfast establishments: it is putting political dogma and posturing before the interests of the homeless and has nothing to do with social justice.

Some may argue that a small alleviation of the awful conditions suffered by the homeless will reduce the pressure for change and thus, in the interests of the homeless, minor improvements should not be attempted. We reject this argument for two reasons.

Firstly, the more people are made to suffer from poor living conditions, the more they become ground down by them and so they are less able to demand and fight for change. Indeed, the analagous logic of such a view is that mass unemployment will cause unstoppable pressure for policy changes—whereas the opposite is true: unemployment causes fear and acquiescence. Homeless people are more able to fight for change if they have one foot on the ladder.

Secondly, this argument involves the cynical manipulation of homeless people for political ends. Outwardly it says: 'This homeless family, Mr and Mrs Smith and their children (real people!) deserve nothing but the best' but behind the scenes the advocates of this policy know that Mr and Mrs Smith are being made to suffer by being left to rot in bed and breakfast for a year because it serves political ends. The constant cry to justify such a policy is that only the best can be provided for the homeless. This in effect means that the homeless remain in bed and breakfast for a year because the best is never available—the 'best' has become the enemy of the 'better'. This, of course, is never explained to Mr and Mrs Smith!

The Green Party's belief in social justice dictates that we do two things: we shout loudly and campaign vigorously and demand that the homeless are provided with high-class permanent accommodation—this book, we hope, does that. At the same time, we do everything in our power to provide the *best possible* accommodation for the homeless *now*. This book is about policies to achieve that—but with two important provisos.

Firstly, the provision of better but inadequate accommodation must only be operated in the interests of the homeless people concerned and never for financial reasons. In other words, while it is justifiable to provide Mr and Mrs Smith with an inadequate short-life home as an alternative to bed and breakfast, it is not justifiable to do so because it is cheaper. This is important because later on (see Chapter 4) we show that emergency housing schemes are, in fact, cheaper. Here, however, in a discussion of principles, this saving is not a relevant consideration.

The second proviso is that any family accommodated in

an emergency home must not suffer any delay or detriment in obtaining permanent rehousing. For our Mr and Mrs Smith, one year in short-term housing may be far preferable to a year in bed and breakfast but they should not be left there any longer than if they had been in bed and breakfast.

The principle of social justice we espouse here ensures the best possible provision for the homeless both now and in the short term, while requiring us to do all in our power to campaign for better housing policies in the middle and long term.

## 2. Environmental Considerations

We must also consider the environment. Here we use that word in the narrow sense to mean the natural environment and we specifically refer to pollution and use of resources.

No policy can ignore environmental issues. Indeed, the environment must always be considered in the interests of those who are affected by the policy. In this case, in the provision of accommodation for the homeless, we must bear the environment in mind in the interest of the homeless themselves. We are not saying that we must, for the sake of the environment, provide perfect 'eco-friendly' accommodation for the homeless, even though that may mean less provision; or that the environment is more important than the homeless; or that, if it is a question of environmentally-damaging accommodation or no accommodation, the Green Party will choose concern for the environment and opt for no accommodation.

We will bear in mind environmental factors and seek as far as possible to provide energy-efficient homes because energy-efficient homes are easier and cheaper to heat. The people living in these homes will be able to afford their rent and so run less risk of becoming homeless again in the future. We are not choosing the environment at the expense of the homeless: we choose to bear environmental factors in mind because it is *in the direct interests of the homeless to do so*.

## 3. Citizen Involvement

Ever since the mid-sixties, when homelessness first became a
national issue, citizen involvement and empowerment has
been central to major developments in the cause of the
homeless.

Central and local government have not effectively dealt
with the problem of homelessness, as witnessed by the
numerous and excellent reports produced by housing charities
and support agencies. We believe the evidence shows
something else too—that government action alone *cannot*
adequately tackle the problem. In the last thirty years, it is
actions by homeless people which have played a crucial role
in bringing about better conditions for the homeless.

Consider the plight of homeless families in the 1960s, so
graphically depicted in the television play *Cathy Come Home*.
Between 1948 and 1965, homeless families were accommodated by social services departments of county councils
under the National Assistance Act 1948. Many councils carried
out their duties under that Act by providing accommodation
for wives and children only—fathers were not allowed to live
with their families. Each year, hundreds of families were
broken up in this way. Some councils put time limits on the
provision of accommodation. This meant that, at the end of
three months, the wives and children were evicted and the
children were forcibly taken into care as there was no shelter
for them. Even more councils provided accommodation in
old workhouses, army barracks, dormitories, illegal caravan
sites, transport cafes and other such 'dumping grounds'.[1]

Despite considerable official condemnation of such
practices, nothing changed until the homeless themselves
took action. In the summer of 1965, Joan Daniels and her
family were due to be evicted from the accommodation
provided by Kent County Council at King Hill hostel (an old
RAF base at West Malling) because Joan and her children had
reached the end of their three month time limit. Joan's husband,
Stan, was not allowed to live with them in the hostel. The

social workers and welfare officials arrived to remove Joan and take her children into care; but they got a shock—for the first time someone stood up to them. Stan Daniels had moved in—and to protect their family Stan and Joan had barricaded the doors! That provided the springboard for a year-long struggle during which seventy more husbands moved in. All the families defied the three-month limit and refused to move and let their children go into care. The authorities reacted with hostility and used every trick and legal tactic they knew to smash the families' resistance. Eviction orders were obtained—and ignored. Injunctions were obtained to stop the husbands visiting their families—and defied. Homeless husbands were jailed for visiting their families. Throughout the year, the families were supported by a small group of political activists—the Friends of King Hill—who organised demonstrations and media coverage.[2] In the end, the battle was won: husbands were allowed to live with their families, the time limit was scrapped and the hostel was greatly improved. Almost overnight many other councils followed suit, fearing a repeat of the trouble. There were other battles about conditions and rules in Essex, Wandsworth and Birmingham[3] where, at one hostel, women were banned from looking out of the window after talking about the appalling conditions to the author of this book and Jeremy Sandford, author of *Cathy Come Home*. Finally, the opposition crumbled after the struggle at King Hill and the showing of *Cathy Come Home* on television. The homeless themselves had won— *despite* the authorities.

At the same time, empty property became an issue. It was obvious (to the homeless) that empty houses could provide better accommodation than the kind of hostels described above. Little was done, however, until a group of homeless people and their supporters occupied some empty houses in the London Borough of Redbridge on 9th February 1969. The battle that followed received national headlines and is dealt with more fully in Chapter 7. Its importance here is that local authorities and the government were only persuaded to take action on empty property after a long and concerted campaign by the homeless themselves. Indeed, even after the events at Redbridge, other long battles followed, in Southwark and Tower Hamlets for instance, to force councils to hand over houses for the use of homeless people.[4] Again, the homeless and their supporters had won in the face of official opposition from all political parties.

The pattern was repeated throughout the 1970s: initiatives to use empty property instead of bed and breakfast; the setting up of hundreds of self-help housing co-operatives to enable homeless single people to take over empty homes; the growth of schemes for ethnic minorities; the provision of hostels for battered and abused women. These ideas came from the homeless and their supporters and all met with varying degrees of suspicion and even hostility from the powers that be.

In the last ten years, the situation has not changed: almost the only provision for single homeless people and childless couples (for which there are no statutory responsibilities) is self-provision—that is, squatting in empty and derelict property. This is particularly the case in inner-city areas. These homeless people have now been declared public enemy number one by the government and many local authorities—but that story is further developed in Chapter 7.

In conclusion, it is our contention that government action has not adequately dealt with homelessness; that it cannot; and that the involvement of the homeless is not only desirable but necessary.

What does this mean for policy?

It certainly does *not* mean that the problem of homelessness simply rests with the homeless and that no government action is required: it *does* mean that strong and effective action by central and local government is essential. As well as action and provision by government, official policies should be designed to involve and encourage homeless people in their widespread efforts to improve their own situations. Government should not only provide—it should also enable. We base our principles not on dogma but on all the available evidence. We reject the Conservative faith in market solutions: these have failed the homeless. We reject the Labour 'statist' solution: it has failed the homeless. Instead, we argue for an extension of the co-operative and self-help activity now taking place. The role of central and local government should be to adopt active and vigorous policies relating both to the provision of housing and to the support of self-help initiatives—a truly mutual aid approach.

**Footnotes**

1. *Cathy Come Home* by Jeremy Sandford, BBC Television play, 1966; *The Grief Report*, Ron Bailey and Joan Ruddock, Shelter, 1972
2. *Kent County County v The Homeless*, Solidarity, 1966
3. *The Squatters*, Ron Bailey, Penguin, 1973
4. ibid.

# 4 Green Party policies

In the next three chapters we explain our policies on homelessness. They involve action by both central and local government. Our policies are based on two essential needs:

• A greatly increased social housing provision over the next few years. There can be no real and lasting solution to the problem of homelessness without a solution to the wider housing problem. A solution to the wider housing problem means that sufficient accommodation of a decent standard, in the right place and at the right price is ensured for all our citizens.* Even if government were totally committed to fulfilling this need, the task is, at best, a medium-term one.

• A crash programme to deal with the problem of homelessness or at least to alleviate it as far as possible. This should be started now while an urgent programme to provide more social housing is being pursued. A crash programme must be able to produce results quickly so that within months, not years, there is renewed hope for as many homeless people as possible and, by next winter, there is a real alternative to freezing on the streets or languishing in overcrowded, dingy bed and breakfast establishments. The policy proposals in this book address this task—a crash programme which will ensure that immediate steps are taken to deal with homelessness.

In Chapter 2, we dealt with empty property: the proper use of empty property can certainly make a major contribution to an immediate crash programme but it cannot solve the housing problem (as some Conservative politicians seem to

*In a future *Policy Pathways* document we will explain the Green Party's policies on this wider issue of housing policy.

think). The government cannot blame empty property for homelessness. The blame rests clearly on inadequate government policies for social housing.

There are certain criteria to be taken into account in the formulation of a homelessness policy. The most important is: can the policy deliver more accommodation now? Our package of measures is designed to answer 'yes' to that question.

Other criteria to be considered are the legal issues and statutory duties which set up a framework within which central and local government policies must give proper consideration to homeless people. Such a framework may not *itself* provide new homes immediately but it will put in place policies which will ensure proper provision in the short and medium term.

**Policy Initiative 1: Extension Of Duties To The Homeless**

In Chapter 1, we saw how duties to provide accommodation for the homeless extend *only* to those in the 'priority classes'. The combination of two factors—the lack of duty and lack of resources—results in provision of accommodation for the non-priority classes playing little part in current policy making, either at central or local government level. This is not to blame local government for we do not doubt that many local councillors and housing officers care deeply about the homeless. However, they have few resources and a massive problem so it tends to be their statutory duties towards the priority classes which drive their policies.

The end result is that pressure is put downwards onto the homeless rather than upwards on the policy and the provision. Whatever the current difficulties, we say that the duty to provide accommodation for the homeless must be extended to the non-priority classes—that is, single people and childless couples. We are realists, however: even if local authorities were given this extension to their duty overnight there would be no chance of them being able to fulfill it straightaway. Therefore, this duty will have to be introduced in stages.

As a first stage, the new duty should be extended immediately to cover sixteen- to eighteen-year olds; in addition, they should be given the right to hold tenancies. The fact that young people are discharged from care onto the streets is unacceptable; the sight of young people sleeping rough cannot be tolerated. A Green council would voluntarily adopt such policies in advance of legislation (which would take about six months to be enacted) and we urge all local authorities to do likewise.

For the remainder of the non-priority classes, legislation extending the duties to cover them should lay down a two- to five-year timetable. This will enable local government to prepare, and central government to provide, the necessary resources. The extension of this duty is the essential first step which will drive future policy.

### Policy Initiative 2: Local Authority Empty Property Strategies

Currently, local authorities have no specific legal duty to ensure the maximum use of empty property and the provision of emergency housing. True, they do have general housing duties concerning the provision of accommodation: The Housing Act 1985, Section 8(1) gives councils a duty to 'consider...the needs of the district with respect to the provision of further housing accommodation.' This duty is based on a similar one in the Housing Act 1957.

However, if this general duty was sufficient, we could reasonably assume that, since 1957, councils would have been maximising the use of empty property to provide emergency accommodation. In practice, of course, this has not been the case: all too often, the homeless have had to fight large scale battles to force councils to use, or permit the use of, empty homes. The evidence in Chapter 2 shows that most councils are still a long way away from making the best possible use of the empty property which they own.

The information given in Chapter 2 does not state why

these homes are empty and for how long they have been empty. It also reveals little about the *potential* that these homes offer. Could any of the existing empty property schemes make beneficial social use of them to provide accommodation for the homeless? Or are new initiatives needed? Without the answers to these questions, little can be done to bring council- and other publicly-owned empty homes into maximum use.

Privately-owned empty houses also present a problem. Although statistics show that large numbers of privately-owned homes are standing empty, a recent Green Party survey reveals that most councils have done nothing to gather the necessary information to enable them to promote schemes to bring these homes into use. Between June and October 1993, we wrote to all housing authorities in England and Wales on the subject of empty privately-owned houses. We had seen that the national statistics, compiled on the basis of the councils' Housing Investment Programme (HIP) returns to the Department of the Environment, indicated that there was a massive problem. We asked the councils for 'any sort of breakdown (eg. time empty, etc.)' of the statistics and also whether they had 'done any surveys or research to find out if any of the privately-owned houses which are still empty can be brought back into use in conjunction with housing agencies for social housing?' This is essential information to enable proper strategies for use to be drawn up.

The replies, printed in Tables 1 and 2, show the extent of inaction by housing authorities on what, as all the official data shows, is a serious problem. Table 1 shows that over three-quarters of councils that replied have no breakdown of the official figures on privately-owned empty homes. Table 2 shows that only a few councils have done further research to find out if empty privately-owned property can be used, despite the fact that many schemes for using such houses already exist. Without this information, pro-active policies to bring more empty homes into use are difficult to achieve.

**Table 1 'Can you give any sort of breakdown (eg. time empty, etc.) of the statistical information on privately-owned empty houses?'**

NO - Adur, Babergh, Barking and Dagenham, Barnsley, Bath, Berwick-upon-Tweed, Birmingham, Blaenau Gwent, Blyth Valley, Boothferry, Bromley, Broxtowe, Bury, Calderdale, Camden, Caradon, Carmarthen, Charnwood, Chesterfield, Chester-le-Street, Cleethorpes, Cotswold, Craven, Croydon, Derbyshire Dales, Derwentside, Dover, East Devon, East Northamptonshire, East Staffordshire, Enfield, Epping Forest, Epsom and Ewell, Forest of Dean, Forest Heath, Glyndwr, Gosport, Greenwich, Guildford, Hammersmith and Fulham, Harrogate, Harrow, Havant, Hertsmere, Hinckley and Bosworth, Hounslow, Hull, Kennet, Kettering, Kingston-upon-Thames, Kingswood, Kirklees, Lambeth, Malvern Hills, Medina, Mendip, Mid Devon, Mid Suffolk, Mole Valley, Newbury, Newcastle-upon-Tyne, New Forest, Northavon, North Tyneside, Norwich, Oldham, Penwith, Preston, Purbeck, Restormel, Ribble Valley, Richmond-upon-Thames, Richmondshire, Rochdale, Rugby, Rushcliffe, Ryedale, St. Edmundsbury, St. Helens, Scarborough, Sevenoaks, Shrewsbury and Atcham, South Bucks, South Herefordshire, South Holland, South Lakeland, South Oxfordshire, South Ribble, Southwark, Stafford, Stockport, Stockton-on-Tees, Stratford-on-Avon, Swayle, Teesdale, Teignbridge, Tendring, Test Valley, Tewkesbury, Vale of Glamorgan, Vale of White Horse, Wakefield, Wansdyke, Waverney, Waverley, Welwyn Hatfield, Wellingborough, West Lancashire, West Oxfordshire, Wigan, Wirral, Wokingham, Wolverhampton, Worcester, Wychavon.

YES - Aberconwy, Aylesbury Vale, Beverley, Brighton, Bristol, Cardiff, Ceredigion, Dudley, Eastbourne, Erewash, Glanford, Haringey, Huntingdonshire, Hyndburn, Ipswich, Lancaster, Leominster, Llanelli, Mansfield, Middlesborough, Northampton, Port Talbot, Solihull, South Cambridgeshire, West Dorset, Woodspring, Wrexham Maelor, Wycombe.

**Table 2 'Have you done any surveys or research to find out if any of the empty privately-owned houses can be brought into use for social housing?'**

**NO** - Aberconwy, Allerdale, Aylesbury Vale, Berwick-on-Tweed, Babergh, Blaenau Gwent, Blyth Valley, Boothferry, Boston, Caradon, Carmarthen, Castle Point, Cheltenham, Chester-le-Street, Chorley, Cleethorpes, Colwyn, Cotswold, Craven, Derwentside, East Cambridgeshire, East Staffordshire, Epsom and Ewell, Forest of Dean, Gosport, Guildford, Harrogate, Havant, Hertsmere, Hinckley and Bosworth, Hull, Kingston-upon-Thames, Kingswood, Lambeth, Meirionnydd, Newark and Sherwood, New Forest, North East Derbyshire, North Tyneside, Restormel, Ribble Valley, Rochdale, St.Edmundsbury, South Herefordshire, South Staffordshire, Staffordshire Moorlands, Tendring, Uttlesford, Vale of White Horse, Wellingborough, West Dorset, Wirral.

**YE - S**Brighton, Bristol, Broxtowe, Bury, Camden, Cardiff, Dover, Eastbourne, Kettering, Langbaugh, Mansfield, Newham, Port Talbot, St.Helens, Stockport, South Oxfordshire, Vale of Glamorgan, Wakefield, Woodspring, Worcester.

The first priority for a Green local authority will be to gather the information on empty property in their area which will enable them to prepare a strategy for maximum use. This will involve finding out what properties are empty; why they are empty; how long they have been empty; how long they are likely to remain empty; and what the possibilities are for use by homeless people, either as short-term or permanent accommodation.

Once this information had been obtained, Green councils would be able to draw up proposals for a variety of schemes to ensure maximum use of all empty homes. These could be for permanent or short-life use (as appropriate) and could involve use by the council itself or by housing associations, community-based groups or self-help groups of homeless

26

people. The whole process should be publicised thus enabling participation by, and suggestions from, all such groups at every stage.

The pioneering examples of a few local authorities show the way for other councils: Southampton City Council, Reading Borough Council, Brighton Borough Council and Mansfield District Council have all adopted comprehensive Empty Property Strategies. Cardiff City Council are about to follow suit.

In Southampton, the scheme was launched in conjunction with the local press and a hot line was set up. The target was a fairly modest 50 lettings in the first year. In fact, 103 empty homes were brought back into use.[1] In Cardiff, the Environmental Services Department drew up a register of empty housing. In March 1993, they had identified 220 privately-owned empty houses that had been vacant for six months or more. On the basis of this information, the Department was able to take action to bring 79 homes back into use.[2]

These initiatives show the value of empty property strategies. A Green local authority would adopt this policy using the Action Pack produced by the Empty Homes Agency as a guide.[3] This document explains in full the pro-active part that council housing, environmental health, planning, legal and financial departments can play. The Green Party calls upon all councils to adopt this policy immediately.

**Policy Initiative 3: Vacant Land Strategies**

Local authorities should embark on a similar process with regard to vacant land. Most publicly-owned land will be listed on a register but there is some evidence that small plots are omitted, often for years.

There is little information held by local authorities on privately-owned vacant land yet this too could be a valuable resource on which to build homes, even on a short-life basis (such as the plans for relocatable, short-life, self-build drawn up for the Diggers Housing Co-operative by Architype[4]).

Private owners may be persuaded to release land they are not proposing to use for some time at fairly nominal rents. A detailed survey undertaken some time ago in the London Borough of Newham revealed considerable potential for self-build homes on many small plots of unused land in the borough. A highway authority with a road scheme planned for five to ten years time should be prevailed upon to allow temporary use of any land acquired in advance.

Proper research and surveys are needed. A Green council would embark upon this task as an immediate priority.

**Policy Initiative 4: Amending Local Plans**

A Green council would amend statutory local plans so that land and buildings could be used in new ways. One recent story illustrates the kind of changes required.

Warwick and Leamington District Council were proposing a new district-wide Local Plan. After lobbying by the local Green Party, they adopted a new planning policy: 'The council will encourage the re-use of empty residential property in order to maximise the availability of the existing housing stock' and, by way of elaboration, the council explained its wish to 'endeavour to work closely with housing associations, the development industry and community groups to ensure that a range of housing is available within the existing housing stock.'[5] This is a simple new policy in which the inclusion of community groups could be of vital importance, in view of some of the proposals contained in this Green Party policy book.

Amendments such as this are not sufficient, however: new forward planning policies will need to be applied to vacant land as well as houses. Green councils will immediately put into operation statutory procedures to secure the necessary amendments to Local Plans. These should prevent future delays—for example, legal challenges—to the Policy Initiatives described below.

## Policy Initiative 5: A Scheme For Reducing Bed and Breakfast Homelessness

One of the most unpleasant aspects of homelessness for families is being placed in 'bed and breakfast'. It can mean living in one room with no cooking facilities and being required to vacate the premises during the day. Families can spend a year in such places, often many miles from their own locality. Family life is impossible and health often suffers. The average weekly cost per family in bed and breakfast is £270 in London and £165 outside London,[6] all paid from public funds. Yet there is a preferable alternative which can provide better (although not necessarily ideal) accommodation at a cheaper price. The important point here is that the accommodation will be *preferable for the homeless*: the saving of money must not be the priority. This policy is driven by the principle of social justice not by financial motives. Indeed, a Green Party council would spend the money saved on other schemes for housing the homeless (see Chapter 5).

The alternative to bed and breakfast involves the use of (often) very short-life empty property to provide accommodation 'in lieu of bed and breakfast'.

This is how it works:

A special housing team is established whose function is to take over and quickly repair empty houses. The houses should be taken over as soon as possible after they become empty as this cuts down on repair bills and obtains the maximum use of the properties, some of which may have as little as six months 'life' before future use or demolition. The team also provides basic furnishing, including bedding and kitchen equipment. It then offers the unit of accommodation to the local authority 'in lieu of bed and breakfast' at a charge which covers all the costs of the unit. The accommodation will be wind- and weather-tight and have a bath or shower and cooking facilities and, if possible, basic heat insulation. It may not meet the local authority's usual housing standards: decoration may not be perfect and it may not be entirely self-contained—for instance, a house may provide two separate units with only one front door and there may possibly still be some overcrowding—but it will be vastly better than bed and breakfast. A short-life home such as this makes the continuation of family life possible and, therefore, it is preferable accommodation for the homeless. However, it is only offered 'in lieu of bed and breakfast': it is *not* offered as permanent accommodation. This point is vital. It is important that families in this accommodation remain there only as long as they would have been in bed and breakfast and then rehoused in permanent accommodation.

Just a good idea? The tragedy is, perhaps, that it is not just an idea: this scheme has worked in practice. It was first proposed by Shelter in 1974[7] and a pilot scheme set up by the author of this book in 1975 under the auspices of London and Quadrant Housing Trust with the backing of its (then) director, Antony Fletcher. At that time, the Trust was acquiring properties for refurbishment or conversion but the process of acquisition, drawing up the specifications, obtaining the necessary approval and so on could take anything between four and twelve months. During this time, these 'pre-contract' properties, as they were known, stood empty. Such a short period of time was of no use to a normal short-life property group (they required the minimum of a year) but it was ideal for 'in lieu of bed and breakfast' purposes.

The Trust took the decision to give all their pre-contract properties a six month 'life' between acquisition (or vacant possession) and the commencement of works. Although this meant that the Trust's own refurbishment works might be delayed for a month or so on some properties, the continued use of the property justified the occasional minor delay. The properties would be handed to the emergency housing section for use 'in lieu of bed and breakfast' for six months. The section would speedily get them ready and offer them to local authorities at about one-quarter the cost of bed and breakfast accommodation. This was higher than a normal weekly rent but the difference enabled the Trust to finance the works required on such very short-life houses. Soon the operation was in full swing and was very successful[8] although not without hiccups—the author of this book was an incompetent housing officer-cum-building supervisor-cum-pressuriser of local authorities and was sacked! Nevertheless, the scheme benefitted homeless families (who had better accommodation than bed and breakfast), local authorities (who saved money with lower costs) and the housing association (with better use of empty property). Antony Fletcher describes its achievements:

'The scheme provided by the Trust in lieu of bed and breakfast accommodation is to offer a home which meets public health standards, including bath or shower and a hot water system, redecorated and provided with basic items of furniture, cooker, electric fire, bedding and floor covering. In 1980/81 the typical weekly charge made by the Trust to the local authority for this service was £40 per flat (inclusive of rates) compared with an average hotel bill then being paid by local authorities per family in bed and breakfast accomodation of some £90 per week. This saving of £50 per week per family, at 1980/81 values, means that local councils, and therefore their ratepayers, had collectively saved over £3m in the six years to 1982, as a result of using this service provided by London and Quadrant Housing Trust.

'The experience gained during the seven years of its existence has enabled the Section to turn an experimental pilot scheme into a professional operation that is foremost in this field. The scheme has never applied for, nor received, any grants and yet is still able to lead the way in what can be done in this field.'[9]

Despite this, only a few housing associations have copied the scheme but, where they have, the results have been similarly successful.

We believe that such a scheme should be expanded. A 'life' of six months is all that is needed for empty houses to be used for emergency accommodation. Given the large number of local authority-owned houses that stand empty for more than six months there would seem to be great potential for emergency housing schemes. Tables 3 and 4 opposite show the statistics.

We can see that, as at April 1st each year, in London there have been over 6,500 council-owned houses that have been empty for more than six months and over 4,000 empty for more than a year. In the country as a whole, over 23,000 council-owned properties have been empty for more than six months and over 15,000 empty for more than a year. The statistics also show two other facts: firstly, *every year* there are many recently vacated dwellings that will remain empty for at least 6 or 12 months (the fact that the figures on empty homes are high from year to year shows this); secondly, we can reasonably assume that the April date is a purely arbitrary date set by the government for statistical reasons. The activity that results in homes becoming and remaining empty does not begin and end in April every year; it is ongoing. *Thus, at any given time, there will be a flow of houses becoming empty that will remain so for at least 6 or 12 months.*

These figures show that there is considerable opportunity for a massive extension of emergency housing schemes 'in lieu of bed and breakfast'. All that is needed is political will. If local authorities had the courage to make the same decision that London and Quadrant Housing Trust made way back in 1975, many of their empty houses could be occupied by homeless people. Councils should give all empty properties in the above categories a six- or twelve-month 'life' before future use, just as London and Quadrant did with its 'pre-contract' properties.

Taking the latest year's figures for London, there are 6,798 properties that could be used for an 'in lieu of bed and breakfast' scheme for six months and 4,469 that could be used for one year. Erring on the side of caution, we will assume that some of these properties could probably not be used (for example, those undergoing major repairs or those in too poor a condition) and with others the six months time vacant will not be predictable. Our estimate, therefore, is that between

**Table 3 Local Authority Vacant Dwellings in London as at 1st April**

Empty more than six months

| Year | Available for letting | To be let after minor repairs | To be let after major works-undergoing repairs | Awaiting repairs | To be sold | Awaitng demolition | Other | Total |
|---|---|---|---|---|---|---|---|---|
| 1992 | 1059 | 1625 | 1270 | 1268 | 515 | 693 | 368 | 6798 |
| 1991 | 1376 | 1336 | 1559 | 1526 | 1045 | 359 | 805 | 8334 |
| 1990 | 1051 | 1168 | 2153 | 1575 | 804 | 275 | 1727 | 9028 |
| **Empty more than 1 year** | | | | | | | | |
| 1992 | 532 | 992 | 790 | 890 | 418 | 560 | 287 | 4469 |
| 1991 | 800 | 732 | 971 | 1190 | 853 | 252 | 562 | 5531 |
| 1990 | 489 | 633 | 1674 | 1295 | 603 | 214 | 1564 | 6623 |

Source: Housing Needs and Resources, compiled by the London Research Centre from HIP submissions

**Table 4 Local Authority Vacant Dwellings Nationally as at 1st April**

Empty more than 6 months

| Year | Available for letting | To be let after minor repairs | To be let after major works-undergoing repairs | Awaiting repairs | To be sold | Awaitng demolition | Other | Total |
|---|---|---|---|---|---|---|---|---|
| 1993 | 2000 | 1700 | 4400 | 2900 | 5500 | 4000 | 2600 | 23000 |
| 1992 | 2400 | 2200 | 4700 | 3800 | 4000 | 5900 | 3600 | 26800 |
| 1991 | 2900 | 3210 | 5500 | 6600 | 5200 | 4400 | 3200 | 31000 |
| **Empty more than 1 year** | | | | | | | | |
| 1993 | 800 | 900 | 2400 | 2000 | 4800 | 3000 | 1900 | 15700 |
| 1992 | 1200 | 2000 | 2600 | 2500 | 3300 | 4300 | 2900 | 18800 |
| 1991 | 1400 | 1600 | 3100 | 4900 | 3900 | 3200 | 2200 | 20200 |

Source: Department of the Environment, annual HIP compilations

2,000 and 2,500 council-owned properties could be 'freed-up' for 'in lieu of bed and breakfast' schemes.

In addition, there are 5,000 vacant housing association homes in London, many of which will remain empty for six to twelve months, yet only a handful of associations are operating the 'in-lieu of bed and breakfast' scheme started in 1975. All housing associations should be required to operate this scheme or to make their empty properties available to it.

Lastly, there are the empty houses owned by government departments. There are two reasons which should make this scheme attractive to such bodies: firstly, the scheme uses houses with a very short life and secondly, the relevant government department can be assured of getting the houses back when required. Empty homes owned by the government should be made available for this scheme immediately.

We believe, therefore, that at a conservative estimate, some 2,500-3,000 publicly-owned empty homes could be made available for such a scheme, either immediately or in a very short period of time, which would provide at least 3,000 units of accommodation.

There are also massive savings to be made from the operation of this scheme. The current average gross cost of keeping a family in bed and breakfast in London is, as we noted above, £14,000 per year or nearly £270 per week. The average cost of the 'in lieu of bed and breakfast' units varies but is around £100 per week.[10] Thus, the provision of better accommodation in lieu of bed and breakfast results in average savings of £170 per week per family. Over a twelve-month period, the 3,000 units that we estimate could be provided in London alone would result in savings of 3,000 x £170 x 52 weeks = £26,520,000. Even allowing for errors and contingencies, savings of at least £20,000,000 could be made. In Chapter 5, we suggest how this money should be spent on further schemes for the homeless.

Outside London, many local authorities also have substantial annual bed and breakfast bills and the empty property statistics in Table 4 show that similar 'in-lieu of bed and breakfast' schemes are possible elsewhere. Indeed, although Table 4 only presents the broad national figures, a detailed investigation of the breakdown authority by authority shows the potential for this scheme in other areas of high bed and breakfast usage.

There are also similar savings to be made. The average weekly cost of bed and breakfast outside London is £165 per week which is slightly under two-thirds of the London cost. Further, the cost of private leasing schemes (whereby councils lease empty privately-owned houses for their own use) is £115 per week outside London as compared with £170 in the capital,[11] again just under two-thirds. Using these figures, we estimate that the average cost of providing 'in-lieu of bed and breakfast' accommodation outside London will be £66 per week, two-thirds of the London figure of £100. Thus, provision of preferable accommodation for homeless families could save councils outside London almost £100 per week per unit.

We believe that this scheme could and be implemented by all local authorities, in conjunction with specialist housing associations and without the help of central government. All it requires is political will. It would, however, be a disgrace if the government failed to respond and did not make its own empty dwellings available for use.

A Green Party local authority would implement such a scheme as follows:

1. We would invite one of the existing emergency housing operations (London and Quadrant Housing Trust, Family Housing Association, West Hampstead Housing Association, etc.) to commence operations in the council's area if they were not already doing so.

2. If necessary, we would assist with establishing a local emergency housing team to run the scheme, possibly with local housing associations. This will be essential outside London. We will actively seek the advice of the London associations operating the scheme.

3. We would take the decision to 'free up' houses owned by the council in the categories listed above (those already

empty and those becoming empty) and give them all a 'life' of 6-12 months before future use.

4. We would call upon local housing associations to do the same with their empty houses, even if they are not running a scheme themselves and we would negotiate with the National Federation of Housing Associations and the Housing Corporation to use their influence to persuade all associations to release vacant homes.

5. We would call upon government departments to release their empty homes and actively campaign against them if they failed to do so.

6. As soon as short-life homes became available, we would place families in them instead of in bed and breakfast. All savings that this achieved would be set aside for spending on other schemes to provide accommodation for the homeless.

The Green Party calls upon all local authorities to embark on this process immediately. We also call upon them to adopt the next policy which is necessary for empty property schemes to be as effective as possible.

**Policy Initiative 6: A Cross-Borough Housing Pool**

The London and Quadrant scheme developed quickly because it was able to use houses according to need without being hidebound by borough boundaries. Units were made available when and where needed to whoever needed them. Borough boundaries are of little relevance to the homeless; technical ownership of empty properties is also irrelevant. To work most effectively, emergency housing schemes should have no such restrictions. Councils should put all empty houses available for short-term occupation into a housing pool for use where needed.

Strangely enough, the call for a cross-borough housing pool was first made by the London Borough of Redbridge in 1969, in response to the occupation of its houses by squatters (see Chapter 7). It was not taken up by the other London

Boroughs. We hope that the publication of this book, on the 25th anniversary of the first squat in council houses in Redbridge, will at last persuade local authorities to adopt this idea.

### Policy Initiative 7: Empty Council Properties— Changing the Presumption on Use

Proven schemes for using empty council-owned property have been in operation for years but, despite these, the statistics show that the problem remains. Any reluctance of councils to hand over their houses may have been understandable (but not justifiable) twenty-five years ago when the first disparate self-help groups of squatters demanded access to empty houses—but any reluctance nowadays is totally inexcusable.

The presumption regarding empty houses must be changed: no longer can it be accepted that a local authority has the right to do what it likes with its (empty) housing stock. A Green council will operate a totally different presumption: any organisation or group that approaches the council to request the use of empty houses owned by the council will be allowed to take over the houses unless the council can show a good reason to the contrary.

In other words, if councils keep homes empty they will lose control of them. A similar idea has been advanced by Conservative MP Hartley Booth in his recent booklet *Into the Voids*.[12] Mr Booth suggests that any individual who spots an empty council-owned house can claim the use of it after a specified time if the council cannot come up with plans to use it. We have some sympathy with this idea but we prefer our scheme because it encourages the establishment of groups rather than individual claims and will, therefore, enable the weaker and less-skilled to have an opportunity to obtain such houses. Our scheme gives access to the houses for the most desperate; Mr Booth's scheme will give access only to the most able.

37

Councils would still retain the right to reject a request for use by a group for 'a good reason'. Examples of good reasons might be: the houses are about to be used; rehabilitation work is due to start shortly (within a specified time); the council has another group in mind for the houses in question; the houses are due to be demolished shortly (within a specified time) for imminent redevelopment (*not* just to leave the space vacant). Other good reasons might be that the council does not consider that the group making the request is capable of using or managing the houses properly; or that they will use the premises for undesirable purposes, for example, to run drug trades.

We include this safeguard because we do not want an example such as the last one, however unusual, to be put forward by councils to attack what is a perfectly sensible policy on presumption-reversal. We have reservations about the safeguard, however, as it could easily be used as a catch-all or prejudiced reason for not handing over houses. In order to minimise that possibility and, more positively, to ensure the best take-up of empty homes, we propose the next Policy Initiative.

## Policy Initiative 8: Developing Self-Help Groups

For twenty-five years, ever since the first 'legal squatting' deals with Lewisham Council in December 1969, self-help groups of homeless people have been successfully operating schemes to use empty houses. Such groups should be encouraged. A Green council would:

(i) publicise to homeless people that the council was drawing up an empty property strategy so that the homeless could take a pro-active role in its preparation;

(ii) give advice and assistance to groups of homeless people to enable them to: establish themselves as capable and efficient self-help housing groups; formulate viable proposals for the use of empty properties; implement their proposals. This will involve employing or redeploying council staff as self-help housing support and development workers;

(iii) assist, promote or set up a specialist secondary housing association in the council's area (if necessary) whose task will be to promote, assist and develop self-help housing groups. We believe that a specialist housing association is necessary because the kind of unofficial arrangements and procedures often adopted by self-help housing groups are best carried out in conjunction with organisations not directly connected with the local authority.

These steps would not only be enormously beneficial (in themselves) in ensuring the maximum use of empty property, they would also minimise, if not eradicate, any abuse of the 'not viable' safeguard in Policy Initiative 7 above. A council could hardly claim that a group was 'not viable' if its own development workers or a specialist secondary housing association had supported the group and played a large part in helping the group to draw up its proposals.

**Policy Initiative 9: Empty Privately-Owned Property—
Action Now**

A number of schemes already exist for bringing empty private property into use for the homeless. These include private sector leasing (councils leasing private houses for use by the council) and housing associations as managing agents (housing associations using private houses to provide accommodation). A Green council will actively promote these. We will stress the benefits to owners and show them examples of good practice in which owners themselves recommend these schemes (see, for example, publications by the Empty Homes Agency and Shelter). The active help of the Empty Homes Agency will be sought.

In addition, a Green local authority, with the agreement of private owners, will not only take over empty houses but also pass them onto self-help groups if the council itself cannot use them, thus acting as a clearing house for such properties. There are many benefits of such an arrangement. Owners are often wary of handing over their houses to groups of (perhaps unorthodox) homeless people but the security of an arrangement with a statutory body should reassure them. For the self-help group there will be advantages, too; often they will not know who the owners are or they may not have the time or the negotiating skills required to persuade owners to hand over houses. The role of the council as intermediary, therefore, could be vital.

In some circumstances, however, a stick may be needed. Some owners are intransigent and care little about the problems caused by their abandoned houses. Such places can become an eyesore and a danger to children; they attract vandals and become unofficial rubbish dumps; they affect the appearance of whole roads and communities; and they are a particular nuisance to neighbours as a result of damp, vandalism and a lessening of security from thieves and burglars.

In such cases, if owners still refuse to permit the use of their empty houses, every action possible will be taken under current law to make it unattractive to leave houses empty. This will include use of the Public Health Acts, nuisance law, dangerous structure laws and the like.

Councils also have powers to compulsorily purchase long-term empty houses and a Green council will seek to use these in appropriate cases. We accept that such action will be limited because of the costs involved (money has to be spent on purchasing the houses) but, by showing the determination to take action, a council will put the owners under further pressure to take the easiest way out and hand over their abandoned houses for use by or for the homeless.

However, indications are that some privately-owned houses are being abandoned to become derelict eyesores and that nothing will persuade the owners to use them or permit their use. We are firmly of the opinion that existing powers are inadequate in such situations and that new powers are needed.

## Policy Initiative 10: Empty Property Use Orders

The statistics quoted in Chapter 2 do not explain the nature of
the problem of long-term empty private houses—those that
are abandoned, neglected or left derelict for many years. It is
in dealing with these houses that existing legal powers are
inadequate.

A few pieces of anecdotal evidence will demonstrate the
problems caused by these houses.

• Take the case of Nos. 8 and 12 Conduit Street, Bristol. In
1987, the Empty Property Campaign, backed by Shelter and
Lord Scarman, reported on these properties. Mr Gerald Davies,
who lived between them at No.10, said: 'I'd rather the
properties were lived in. It would stop the fall in value of my
property. I'd like to buy the properties from the owner and
my bank is willing to give me a loan to do up the properties
but I can't trace the owner. The houses are over 100 years old.
They are good houses and structurally very sound. I've had
no problems with mine apart from the damp from next door
(No.12).'[12] Seven years later the properties are still empty.

• Bristol Council have even been petitioned by neighbours
complaining of the effects of empty property. The residents of
the Henleaze area wrote that 'the following have contributed
to a deplorable situation:-

    (a) House unoccupied since June 1979, and contents,
        including not only furniture and clothes, but also
        food, which having been left since that date could
        create a health hazard.

    (b) Fences broken down, trees and shrubs unattended,
        and garden totally overgrown, is causing a nuisance
        to neighbours both adjacent and at the rear.

    (c) Windows broken, and evidence of vagrants.

    (d) *The owner is indifferent to all approaches made*, and it
        isnow=in such a disgusting state residents are having
        difficulty in disposing of their property.'[14]

All political parties on Bristol City Council are united in
the call for action on such properties and have supported the

use of compulsory purchase orders. However, as Labour Housing Chairperson, Councillor George Micklewright, has stated: 'The problem of using CPOs is that the procedure is long-winded and it is very much a last resort. It's like using a sledgehammer. But at present we have no alternative if persuasion does not work. We could do with something more sophisticated and wieldy than CPOs. The use of Empty Property Use Orders (EPUOs) would help to make our policy more effective. They would not take so long as CPOs and we could intervene a lot sooner.'[15]

His Conservative opposite number, Councillor Terry Allen, has taken a similar view, saying that: 'Some of the places are falling down brick by brick. They even become a danger. It was brought home to us by the housing situation that something needed to be done so we backed the scheme. Our philosophy normally would be not to intervene against private property, and we do have some sympathy for the owners. But we have more sympathy for the neighbours having to endure these empty properties nearby and for the potential occupants. The idea of EPUOs appeals to us. They will give us another, less drastic, power to help us secure use of these long-term empty houses. The new power could even lessen the need for extreme CPO actions.'[16]

• A classic example of the need for EPUOs is the block of 400 empty flats in Artillery Row, Victoria, London, mentioned in Chapter 2. The owners have resisted all pleas for short-term use; they have planning permission for development in the future and yet the flats have been allowed to fall into disrepair for years. A compulsory puchase order would be prohibitively expensive and inappropriate in view of the planning permission. An EPUO, or even the threat of it, could secure the use of these flats for up to five years without harming anybody's long-term interest.

These flats are the type of long-term empty property we are concerned with here: homes that have stood empty for years, despite all efforts to secure their use. Existing legal powers have proved ineffective so new powers are needed:

we therefore propose the introduction of Empty Property Use Orders. These would give local authorities the power to take over *long-term* empty houses for up to five years and use them for homeless people.

We are aware that many people who are concerned about empty houses will feel considerable reticence about giving councils powers over privately-owned properties. We share this reticence so we shall explain in detail why we believe EPUOs are, in certain circumstances, justifiable.

## (1) EPUOs Are Not Draconian

EPUOs can only be served on *long-term* empty properties; they cannot be put on houses left empty while being sold or while the owners are on holiday (see the Homeless Persons and Mutual Aid Bill in Chapter 6). There are also built-in safeguards in the EPUO procedure and these, too, are explained in detail in Chapter 6. As Lord Scarman has said: 'This is not an appropriation measure—it distinguishes between use and ownership.'[17] However, the argument against those who believe that it is a draconian power does not end there. There are three legal points to consider:

(a) The power to put EPUOs on empty properties is a *lesser* power than exists already. Some councils (for example, the Royal Borough of Kensington & Chelsea, Bristol City Council, Reading Borough Council and Mansfield District Council) have put Compulsory Purchase Orders (CPOs) on empty property and these have been approved by the Department of the Environment. CPOs allow total expropriation of the properties by the Council forever. EPUOs only permit a Council to use a house for up to five years and then it must be returned it to the owner (in better condition probably!). Indeed, it is precisely because councils do not currently have EPUO powers that CPOs are more likely to be used—as the Bristol Conservative councillor, Terry Allen, has already made clear.

(b) In the case of properties deemed unfit for human

habitation, or houses falling into rack and ruin, councils can also declare them unfit, thereby making the use of them a criminal offence. The councils can then CPO them at site value only. Once again, this is a far more extreme power than an EPUO.

(c) Local authorities already have powers equivalent to an EPUO: they can put control orders on houses in multi-occupation. A control order enables a council to take over such houses for five years where conditions affect 'the safety, health or welfare' of the occupants. An EPUO simply applies the same principle to empty properties since they can also become a risk to the safety, health and welfare of neighbours, nearby residents and indeed whole neighbourhoods.

For these reasons, therefore, we feel it is incorrect to describe the EPUO powers as draconian.

## (2) Benefits To Residents, Neighbours and Neighbourhoods

The stories above amply demonstrate that long-term empty houses create problems not only for people living nearby but also the whole neighbourhood. Note the words of the DoE Inspector describing some abandoned houses in a Conservation Area in the London Borough of Kensington & Chelsea: he stresses 'the highly detrimental effect of the properties on nearby properties' and notes that 'the two properties (in question) are virtually derelict.'[18]

Worry, distress, damp, danger, fires, ill health, unsightly gardens, loss of property values, dereliction of property in Conservation Areas, neighbourhoods spoilt; these problems are suffered by the whole community when properties are allowed to lie empty, abandoned and derelict.

It is because of exceptional circumstances such as these that local authority intervention is justified. As the law stands at present, the 'final' power is the very drastic CPO: an EPUO gives a less drastic but more flexible weapon with which to counter these problems.

## (3) Benefits To Ratepayers

EPUOs can directly benefit ratepayers by saving money.
• Take the example of Lockside Cottages, Narrow Street, E14 in the London Borough of Tower Hamlets. These are six houses owned by the British Waterways Board (BWB) and left empty for twenty-three years. Numerous requests for use have been turned down by the BWB.

Meanwhile, Tower Hamlets Council has spent vast sums on bed and breakfast accommodation. If these six houses had been EPUO'd years ago and used for homeless families, either by the Council or by a housing association, vast savings of public money would have resulted.

Six units of EPUO'd property for five years would have cost:

| | |
|---|---|
| Initial repairs at say £15,000 per home | £90,000 |
| Ongoing maintenance, say £1,000 per house per annum (£1,000 x 6 houses x 5 years) | £30,000 |
| Management costs, say 1/10 annual salary of £14,000 (£1,400 x 5 years) | £7,000 |
| Miscellaneous | £3,000 |
| **Total** | **£130,000** |

Six family units of bed and breakfast for five years would have cost:

| | |
|---|---|
| 6 units x £270 per week x 260 weeks | **£421,200** |

Therefore the saving to ratepayers would have been:
$$£421,200 - £130,000 = £291,200$$

Even allowing for some 'void' weeks in the use of the properties between one family vacating and another occupying, the nett benefit to the ratepayers would still be at least £250,000. Similar calculations can be applied to hundreds of long-term empty houses in many areas and the money saved could be spent on other schemes for the homeless (see Chapter 5).

## (4) Benefits to the Homeless

For homeless families, bed and breakfast is nasty: it is often overcrowded, dangerous and dirty. Family life is impossible—yet families may spend years in such accommodation. Living in an EPUO'd property would be a vast improvement.

The single homeless would also benefit from EPUOs. Under the proposed Homeless Persons and Mutual Aid Bill (see Chapter 6) these people could join together to get permission from local authorities to renovate EPUO'd houses for their own use. This would provide homes, employment, hope and restored self-respect for the single homeless and jobless.

## (5) Benefit to Owners

At present, owners lose their properties for good after CPO actions. An EPUO may well be preferable: the owner would lose the use (or non-use!) of her/his house for five years but would get it back in better condition thereby improving its value and making it easier to sell.

We believe that EPUOs are both necessary and justified. Therefore, we intend to launch and campaign for all-party support for Empty Property Use Orders which will be introduced in our Homeless Persons and Mutual Aid Bill.

### Policy Initiative 11: Self-Build and Publicly-Owned Vacant Land - Combined Central and Local Government Action

Unknown to many people, numerous plots of land exist which lie unused and vacant for years. These plots are owned by councils and other public bodies. They are officially classed as 'unused' or 'underused' or 'surplus to requirements' and listed as such on a public register.

The use of this land by and for homeless people has been totally overlooked until now and yet it offers an opportunity to provide a large number of homes.

Under Part X of the Local Government Planning and Land Act 1972, all councils are required by law to keep a register (a list) of vacant or underused and surplus land owned by themselves and by other public bodies. These registers are known as Part X registers. They contain details of all the surplus land, its size, why it was acquired and a brief statement of intended use in the future. The land is publicly owned and it is vacant: we say, therefore, that it is a resource that can be used to provide homes for homeless people.

The plots vary greatly in size and topography and not all land on the register will be suitable for housing. A plot 'acquired for housing purposes' can reasonably be assumed to be suitable for homes but another plot, listed simply as 'development land', may well lie between two gasworks and so may not be suitable. Similarly, we would be reluctant to suggest that land currently listed on the Part X register as 'unused allotments' should be used for housing as we recognise the social, environmental (and nutritional) value of allotments.

The policy of a Green council regarding the land in the Part X registers would be:

(i) to use all land classed as housing land to provide homes for homeless people;

(ii) to transfer all land held as development land or industrial land to housing purposes *where appropriate*. In other words, there would be a presumption in favour of transfer;

(iii) not to transfer allotment land unless there was a good reason for so doing (for example, no demand for allotments). In other words, there would be a presumption against transfer.

**How Much Land ?**

The only way to answer this question is to examine the Part X registers. We collected over 120 of them from local authorities all over the country, ranging from inner-city areas of London to small towns and rural areas. We listed the land designated

47

as housing land and assumed that this land could and should be used for housing schemes for the homeless.

We followed up the other sites by writing to some councils asking them about the *suitability* of using these sites for housing (as opposed to their current policies). In other cases, we used the background information on the registers to make an assessment as to the suitability of the land for housing purposes. In Chapter 5, we present detailed results of this exercise, area by area. Here we simply report our findings that there is a considerable amount of vacant or surplus publicly-owned land that is suitable for use as housing land.

A Green local authority would declare all this land no longer surplus and no longer vacant. It would designate these sites as 'land to be used for emergency housing provision' and would ensure that schemes were put into the pipeline immediately.

## How?

Having established the availability of land, a Green council would then embark upon the task of ensuring that the homes are built. We seriously doubt that councils could build the homes; we also question whether it is desirable that councils should do it all themselves, even if they had the resources. A Green council would certainly wish to be an active enabler, adviser and supporter of schemes to build on vacant land: it would not, however, necessarily wish to build the houses itself (although we do not rule out direct provision by local authorities). A Green council would get the job done via self-build schemes. This would involve homeless people drawing up plans, designing, approving and then building homes on the land to provide cheap, high-standard, rented accommodation for the homeless.

Is this possible? There are two answers to that. Firstly, the same doubts were cast about the viability of homeless people taking over empty properties in 1969 when Lewisham London Borough Council first handed houses over to squatters (see

Chapter 7). Since then, and directly as a result of that action, self-help schemes have spread and have been operating successfully for twenty-five years. Secondly, successful self-build for rent schemes already exist and they work. [19]

Let us look at one example in some detail to explain how it can happen:

In South East England, a secondary housing association, known as CHISEL, is sponsoring a number of self-build for rent projects in conjunction with a specialist self-build design consultancy called Architype. CHISEL report that 'self-build for rent is no longer a pipe dream, but an exciting new model for the production of social housing.'[20] The CHISEL model has been developed within current Housing Corporation procedures and so does not require 'special conditions which might be difficult to recreate.'[21]

CHISEL's schemes are funded by money from the Housing Corporation known as Housing Association Grant (HAG). This money is available to housing associations registered with the Corporation, usually the larger and more 'official' associations. Small self-help groups of homeless people can easily form themselves into housing associations or co-operatives, but not ones registered with the Corporation, so they themselves cannot get direct access to HAG money. However, legitimate ways have been found to get round this: the association registered with the Corporation obtains the HAG money for the self-build scheme and uses the money to employ CHISEL as a development agent for the scheme. CHISEL's job is to ensure that the homes are built.

To do this, CHISEL in turn enters into an agreement with a self-build housing co-operative. CHISEL's agreement with this co-operative is that the co-operative agree to build the houses specified and CHISEL uses the HAG money to pay them a notional contract sum in return for doing so. When the houses are finished, the members of the housing co-operative rent them from the co-operative and live in the homes that they themselves have built.

Who are the self-builders and co-operative members? As CHISEL explains, they work 'very closely with the local authority in order to identify the most appropriate' people.[22] 'Some councils will wish to canvass their waiting lists for potential co-operative members. Others might want to target particular groups like ethnic minorities or homeless single people. In all such cases, CHISEL will help set up the group so that they become an able self-build co-op.'[23] In other words, the members of the housing co-operative will be a group of homeless people who have registered as a housing co-operative under the Industrial and Provident Societies Act 1965. Such a process is extremely simple and costs only about £200. In this way, government money from the Housing Corporation can be channelled through the more official housing associations via CHISEL to self-help groups of homeless people.

The self-build schemes which have been set up using this procedure have worked very well. CHISEL's input into the schemes, in terms of advice and support, has been a crucial factor. Indeed, as their own publication stresses: 'one of our responsibilities in getting these schemes off the ground is ensuring that prospective self-builders are encouraged and trained, not only in building, but also in site organisation and co-operative management.'[24]

Such back-up is a big part of the equation, as is expert knowledge on site. There may be jobs that a self-build co-operative cannot do and specialist consultants are needed to advise on these. Indeed, CHISEL requires that the self-build co-operative must employ a skilled Contract Manager with building and construction experience. Self-build means that most of the work is done by the group and the group retains control: it does not mean that every group of homeless people has to do everything. The group may need specialists and managers but these will be their specialists and managers and employed by them.

## Funding and Costs

The total costs of providing the homes are made up of three elements: acquisition of the land; the notional amount of money that it will take to carry out the works required; and other miscellaneous costs known as 'on costs'.

The land cost element is the cost of purchasing the land and we will say more about that later.

The notional cost is the amount of money at which CHISEL notionally contracts the self-build co-operative to build the homes. This will include the cost of materials and the notional labour costs. The latter cost is notional because, of course, the labour is free. The notional figure is included because the self-builders are repaid for their labour by being given loan stock in the scheme when the houses are finished. The notional cost is calculated according to an established formula based upon the cost per square meter of housing space provided. CHISEL's scheme in Brighton, for instance, is based upon a notional cost of £610 per square meter of floor area.

The miscellaneous or 'on costs' element includes consultants fees, administration fees and other costs.

The notional costs of the Brighton scheme are calculated in Table 5.

### Table 5  Costs of CHISEL Scheme

| | |
|---|---|
| Land acquisition at market value | £125,000 |
| Notional contract costs (513 sq m x £610) | £312,930 |
| On costs | £ 87,911 |
| **Total notional costs** | **£525,841** |

In fact, the actual contract costs are £232,980 rather than the notionally allowed amount of £312,930, so the total actual costs are £445,891. The difference represents the effort of labour put in by the self-builders. The scheme involves 9 units providing homes for 33 people (5x5-person units and 4x2-

person units) This means that each unit of self-build includes a labour element of £8,883.33 (£312,930 - £232,980 ÷ 9) and this amount would be the average loan stock issued when the scheme has been completed.

The scheme has two further advantages worth noting. Firstly, the accommodation provided is extremely good quality but is within Housing Corporation cost limits so it represents good value for money in any terms. Secondly, and more importantly, the housing co-operative is able to charge its members cheap and affordable rents.

We have seen that the total actual costs are £445,891. The grant made available to the scheme (the HAG money) will be £387,760 for the 33 persons accommodated (or just over £11,500 per bed space). The difference is the amount that the housing co-operative has to borrow, in this case £58,131 or £6,459 per property. The weekly payments on such a mortgage by the housing co-operative (note, individual members do not have to be personally 'mortgage-worthy') will be about £10 per week per property. This will be collected from the rents charged.

The total rent that the co-operative will need to charge its members will be:

| | |
|---|---|
| Management | £4.21 |
| Maintenance | £5.42 |
| Major repair allowance | £12.96 |
| Ongoing training | £1.50 |
| Loan repayment | £10.31 |
| Loan stock reserve | £3.60 |
| | |
| **Total** | **£38.00 per week** |

This is a cheap rent, well within social security limits. As CHISEL says: 'In effect the labour contributed by the self-builders (and represented in the loan stock) replaces most of the private borrowing required. Rents can therefore be set at genuinely affordable levels.'[24]

The idea that a local authority would hand over land *en masse* to ad hoc groups of homeless people to enable them to build their own homes may be alien to those who see solutions in terms of 'market forces' or 'local authority provision'. However, though the scheme described above is novel, it shows that there is a Green alternative which works in practice.

A Green council will develop and streamline this model. Our procedure will be as follows:

1. Immediate identification of land suitable for housing by the local authority from the Part X registers, according to the criteria explained above. This land will be guaranteed.

2. Any necessary planning procedures put in motion to avoid possible future delays - see Policy Initiative 4 above.

3. Immediate establishment of CHISEL-type teams in each area. These can be local authority workers or teams established under the auspices of an existing local housing association or by the setting up of a specialist, secondary housing association like CHISEL. Existing associations and consultants will be contracted to advise the council on how to expedite this process.

4. Publicising and promotion of the scheme locally, particularly among the homeless, and an invitation to individuals and groups to come forward to receive advice and support and to register as housing co-operatives under the Industrial and Provident Societies Act 1965.

5. Active seeking of a Housing Corporation-registered housing association willing to apply for the HAG money and operate the scheme.

It is obvious that the amount of land a Green council would make available and the number of schemes it would seek to start will mean that current Housing Corporation funding will be nowhere near sufficient. So what can be done?

We believe that *central government should provide the money to fund these schemes*. Although they involve a considerable amount of money, these schemes also offer value for money for a number of reasons. Firstly, the costs of providing the units in the CHISEL model are less than Housing Corporation costings. Secondly, homeless people sleeping rough are usually unemployed. Assisting them with self-build housing schemes will teach them new skills and enhance their abilities, thereby enabling them to get back into the labour market. Thirdly, the government could agree to provide the funding if the local authority provided the land free of charge: this would take out the land acquisition costs included in our model above. We regard this as a fair partnership for combined central and local government action. The provision of the land free of charge would reduce the cost per bed space from just over £11,000 to around £10,000. The government should also do everything in its power to secure the release of 'other public land' on the Part X registers which is owned by government departments and quangos.

The crux of the matter is whether central government has the political will to pursue a policy to eradicate homelessness. We have demonstrated what is possible and what constitutes value for money: we call upon the government to respond. Below we suggest two policy initiatives that could help considerably in the funding of these schemes which would cost the government nothing.

## Policy Initiative 12: Release of Local Authority Reserves

The sale of council houses has meant that local authorities have received large sums of money paid to them by buyers. These reserves are currently frozen—by government edict: councils are not allowed to spend any of this money because of central government regulations. In order for the emergency programme on homelessness to proceed effectively, central government must release this money immediately.

## Policy Initiative 13: Mortgage Tax Relief

Mortgage tax relief is automatically claimed when people become home-owners. It is not a need-based tax relief and costs the government billions of pounds each year in revenue.

The Green Party's principles of social justice dictate that this money should be redirected towards the homeless and others in housing need (including home-owners on a need-assessed basis) rather than towards home-owners simply *by virtue* of their home ownership. The phasing out of mortgage tax relief would produce a large amount of tax revenue: this should be spent on the schemes we have outlined here and other housing initiatives for the homeless. This would be revenue neutral; it only involves a policy decision which should be taken at once. We call upon the government to take this decision.

**Footnotes**

1. Empty Homes Agency Booklet, 1993
2. Letter to Green Party from Cardiff City Council, 1.11.93
3. *Empty Property Strategies*, Empty Homes Agency, 1993
4. *Relocatable Self-Build Houses*, Architype Design Co-operative (for Diggers Self-Build Housing Co-operative)
5. Warwick and Leamington Draft District Plan
6. Figures compiled by Shelter from information from CIPFA
7. *Bed and Breakfast*, Ron Bailey, Shelter, 1974
8. *The Homeless and the Empty Houses*, Ron Bailey, Penguin, 1977
9. *Homes Wasted*, Antony Fletcher, Shelter, 1982
10. Information from London and Quadrant Housing Trust, December 1993
11. Figures supplied by Shelter from information from CIPFA
12. *Into the Voids*, Hartley Booth MP, Adam Smith Institute, 1993
13. *Empty Property Use Orders*, Campaign for An Act of Parliament, 1987
14. ibid.
15. ibid.
16. ibid.
17. ibid.
18. Inspector's Report, Royal Borough of Kensington and Chelsea (Vacant Properties) CPO, 1986

19. *Self-Build for Rent*, Jose Ospina, CHISEL, 1992
20. ibid.
21. ibid.
22. ibid.
23. ibid.
24. ibid.

# 5 What a Green Council would do: a costed strategy

We stated in Chapter 4 that action by central government is both desirable and necessary if the policies we have advocated are to be most effective. Some of the policy initiatives can only be taken by central government—the release of council reserves, the ending of mortgage tax relief, taking the political decision to make sufficient money available, and formulating a housing policy that will provide enough homes to solve the problem of homelessness. Other initiatives involve Parliamentary action—for example, The Homeless Persons and Mutual Aid Bill in Chapter 6. However, we accept the political reality that this government may not respond as we would wish; their track record is evidence of this. Shelter, the Campaign for the Homeless and Rootless (CHAR) and other influencial national organisations have been calling for more action for years without obtaining a satisfactory response.

A Green council will tackle the problem of homelessness head on. *We will not allow government inaction to disempower us*. A Green local authority will find ways round all the rules, regulations and bureaucracy in order to implement our policies. We will demonstrate that it is possible, even in the face of government inertia, for local authorities to take effective action by themselves.

**Policy Initiative 14: Vacant Land, Homelessness and Mutual Aid**

Here we describe what *councils* can do *now*. We realise that real action is far more effective if carried out by groups of local authorities so a Green council would seek the co-operation of other local authorities to carry out these policies.

There are four hurdles to overcome in order to achieve the large-scale provision of accommodation we envisage:

1. where the accommodation can be built (on what land);
2. where the money is coming from (assuming no government help);
3. the nature of the homes (environmental considerations);
4. how the homes can be built.

## 1. Land

All local authorities are required by law to keep a Part X register of vacant and surplus publicly-owned land. Some of this land is suitable for housing. In order to find out how much housing land there is, we obtained Part X registers from a sample of 120 local authorities.

Using the method and the criteria described in Policy Initiative 11, we then made two calculations: the amount of land suitable for housing and the amount of land *possibly* suitable for housing. We added the total area of land suitable for housing to *half* of the total area of land possibly suitable for housing (thus allowing for a wide margin of error). In this way we arrived at an assessment of the amount of land available for housing in each local authority area. These figures are, of course, broad estimates: each council will need to carry out its own detailed investigation to arrive at exact figures. The results show that there is an enormous amount of publicly-owned land which could be used to build homes for homeless people and, since this land is situated not only in inner cities but also in small towns and rural areas, that it is available throughout the country.

In Tables 1, 2 and 3 we list the amount of surplus publicly-owned land that is available for our scheme using the method of calculation above.

# A COSTED STRATEGY

## Table 1  London Boroughs (14 registers obtained)

| Borough | Suitable for housing (acres) | Possibly suitable for housing (acres) | Total acres (col.1 + 50% col.2) |
|---|---|---|---|
| Barking and Dagenham | 43.94 | 58.66 | 73.27 |
| Bromley | 3.51 | - | 3.51 |
| Croydon | 1.34 | 1.59 | 2.135 |
| Greenwich | 5.10 | 17.80 | 14.00 |
| Hammersmith and Fulham | - | - | - |
| Hillingdon | 14.50 | 10.80 | 19.90 |
| Hounslow | 0.75 | - | 0.75 |
| Lambeth | 1.25 | 2.39 | 2.445 |
| Richmond-upon-Thames | 6.13 | - | 6.13 |
| Southwark | 9.4 | 4.19 | 11.515 |
| Sutton | - | 2.10 | 1.05 |
| Tower Hamlets | 5.97 | 2.28 | 7.11 |
| Wandsworth | - | 12.74 | 6.37 |
| Westminster | - | - | - |

## Table 2  Metropolitan Boroughs (9 registers obtained)

| Borough | Suitable for housing (acres) | Possibly suitable for housing (acres) | Total acres (col.1 + 50% col.2) |
|---|---|---|---|
| Birmingham | 60.67 | 17.63 | 69.48 |
| Bolton | 40.57 | 49.37 | 65.25 |
| Coventry | 67.97 | 37.77 | 86.85 |
| Rochdale | 13.00 | 35.38 | 30.69 |
| Sefton | 6.50 | 225.71 | 119.35 |
| Solihull | 0.00 | 0.00 | 0.00 |
| Wakefield | 152.93 | 36.47 | 171.65 |
| Wirral | 32.34 | 48.75 | 56.71 |
| Wolverhampton | 2.24 | 10.92 | 7.70 |

## Table 3 Shire Districts (97 registers obtained)

| Authority | Suitable for housing (acres) | Possibly suitable for housing (acres) | Total acres (col.1 + 50% col.2) |
|---|---|---|---|
| Amber Valley | 11.22 | - | 11.22 |
| Ashford | 0.84 | 0.25 | 0.965 |
| Babergh | 2.00 | - | 2.00 |
| Bassetlaw | 45.55 | 10.16 | 50.63 |
| Bath | 0.83 | 4.71 | 3.185 |
| Blackburn | 19.73 | - | 19.73 |
| Bolsover | 32.85 | 2.55 | 34.125 |
| Brentwood | 3.08 | 0.86 | 3.51 |
| Burnley | 12.03 | 4.93 | 14.495 |
| Carlisle | 3.35 | 1.47 | 4.085 |
| Castle Morpeth | 28.86 | 3.82 | 30.77 |
| Cheltenham | - | 10.63 | 5.315 |
| Chester-le-Street | 0.67 | - | 0.67 |
| Christchurch | - | 3.84 | 1.92 |
| Cleethorpes | 1.80 | - | 1.80 |
| Colchester | 27.67 | 2.32 | 28.83 |
| Crawley | 3.60 | 9.70 | 8.45 |
| Dartford | 8.36 | 2.20 | 9.46 |
| East Hampshire | 3.36 | 3.91 | 5.315 |
| Epping Forest | 8.31 | - | 8.31 |
| Exeter | 2.18 | 0.27 | 2.315 |
| Gillingham | 14.35 | - | 14.35 |
| Glanford | 1.60 | 39.03 | 21.115 |
| Great Grimsby | 2.15 | 0.50 | 2.40 |
| Hartlepool | 1.10 | 1.44 | 1.82 |
| Hastings | 39.41 | - | 39.41 |
| Hinckley and Bosworth | 6.62 | 2.38 | 7.81 |
| Holderness | 12.85 | - | 12.85 |
| Horsham | 9.50 | - | 9.50 |
| Hyndburn | 76.10 | 1.70 | 76.95 |
| Ipswich | 7.56 | 1.87 | 8.495 |
| Kennett | 6.05 | - | 6.05 |
| Kettering | 14.22 | - | 14.22 |
| Leominster | 0.33 | 0.69 | 0.675 |
| Lichfield | - | 2.73 | 1.365 |

# A COSTED STRATEGY

| Authority | Suitable for housing (acres) | Possibly suitable for housing (acres) | Total acres (col.1 + 50% col.2) |
|---|---|---|---|
| Luton | - | 2.33 | 1.165 |
| Medina | 2.54 | 28.28 | 16.68 |
| Mendip | 3.00 | - | 3.00 |
| Mid Devon | - | 4.76 | 2.38 |
| Middlesborough | 51.51 | - | 51.51 |
| Mid Suffolk | 21.44 | 4.30 | 23.59 |
| Northavon | 113.83 | 14.56 | 121.11 |
| N.Norfolk | 24.68 | 19.27 | 34.315 |
| N.W.Leicestershire | 11.20 | 21.96 | 22.18 |
| Norwich | 4.77 | 8.44 | 8.99 |
| Nuneaton and Bedworth | 36.05 | - | 36.05 |
| Oadby and Wigston | 0.46 | - | 0.46 |
| Penwith | 27.92 | 38.91 | 47.375 |
| Preston | 9.49 | 1.96 | 10.47 |
| Rushmoor | 0.76 | 5.68 | 3.60 |
| Shrewsbury and Atcham | 1.16 | 8.64 | 5.48 |
| Southampton | 12.84 | 5.82 | 15.75 |
| S.Lakeland | 46.00 | 2.92 | 47.46 |
| S.Norfolk | 12.39 | 19.16 | 21.97 |
| S.Oxfordshire | - | 0.70 | 0.35 |
| S.Shropshire | 39.67 | 1.70 | 40.52 |
| Stafford | 2.27 | 7.84 | 6.19 |
| Staffordshire Moorlands | 1.05 | - | 1.05 |
| Stevenage | 0.60 | - | 0.60 |
| Stratford-on-Avon | 5.29 | - | 5.29 |
| Stroud | 15.80 | 5.05 | 18.325 |
| Suffolk Coastal | 35.42 | 31.61 | 51.225 |
| Surrey Heath | 8.56 | - | 8.56 |
| Tandridge | 16.08 | 1.00 | 16.58 |
| Teignbridge | 11.94 | - | 11.94 |
| Thurrock | 12.50 | 14.30 | 19.65 |
| Tonbridge and Malling | - | 5.90 | 2.95 |
| Torbay | 1.98 | 24.18 | 14.07 |
| Uttlesford | 0.18 | - | 0.18 |
| Waveney | 2.68 | - | 2.68 |
| Wealdon | 5.22 | - | 5.22 |
| Wear Valley | 16.15 | - | 16.15 |

| Authority | Suitable for housing (acres) | Possibly suitable for housing (acres) | Total acres (col.1 + 50% col.2) |
|---|---|---|---|
| Welwyn and Hatfield | 12.38 | 0.07 | 12.415 |
| West Dorset | 3.07 | - | 3.07 |
| West Lancashire | 3.41 | - | 3.41 |
| Weymouth and Portland | 9.58 | - | 9.58 |
| Woking | 3.64 | 3.86 | 5.57 |
| Wokingham | 18.98 | - | 18.98 |
| Worthing | 5.87 | 0.38 | 6.06 |
| Wycombe | - | 12.72 | 6.36 |
| Wyre Forest | 15.98 | 1.37 | 16.665 |

Let us look at the information in the Tables in more detail. In Table 1 (London) the total figure in column three of 148 acres is the area of publicly-owned land that we have calculated is available for housing from the 14 registers that we obtained. There are 32 boroughs in London (excluding the City of London) and if we assume a similar spread of land throughout the boroughs, we can estimate a total of 338 acres to be available in London. Here, however, we will err on the side of caution and reduce this to a round figure of 300 acres. The typical planning density for the type of housing we would be building is 75 habitable rooms per acre. Therefore, 300 acres would allow for the construction of 22,500 habitable rooms (300 acres x 75 rooms per acre). In planning terms, habitable rooms include all bedrooms, a living-room and a kitchen over a certain size. A two-bedroomed unit will have 3 or 4 habitable rooms (depending on the size of the kitchen) and a three-bedroomed unit, 4 or 5 habitable rooms. If we assume, for the purpose of this broad general outline, that we are building three-bedroomed homes with 5 habitable rooms at a density of 75 rooms per acre, the number of homes we could build on each acre is 15, comprising at least 45 bed spaces for at least 45 homeless people. (This type of shared house is typical of the provision for single homeless people in self-build schemes and is very popular.) Therefore, on 300 acres of land in London, we could build 4,500 homes (15 per acre) and provide housing for at least 13,500 people (3 bed spaces per home x 4,500 homes).

In practice, of course, the homes would vary in size according to local demands and preferences. The accommodation provided would also probably house more people as shared rooms are common in these schemes. We put forward this basic model to show that there is sufficient vacant public land to provide homes for a large number of homeless people.

Tables 2 and 3 show that there is also a large amount of vacant land outside London which could be used for housing for homeless people. The same method can be applied to estimate the number of homes that could be provided and the number of people that could be accommodated for each local authority area.

The best way to proceed in the local authority areas listed in Tables 2 and 3 would be on a county-wide basis, as this would ensure some provision for the homeless in those areas where we have not identified any Part X land as being suitable: Arun, Broxbourne, Chichester, Eastleigh, Maldon, Purbeck, Richmondshire, Rochford, Slough, South Beds, South Ribble, Teesdale, Warwick and Leamington, Waverley, and Windsor and Maidenhead.

Table 4 (below) shows how much land could be available in the old metropolitan county areas. This is calculated using the total figure from Table 2 of 607.68 acres (from nine registers)—an average of 67.52 per metropolitan borough. Erring on the side of extreme caution we have more than halved this to 25 acres per borough, and then applied this average to the former metropolitan county areas. We stress that this is a very rough calculation, subject to a wide margin of error, and that local authorities will need to carry out further detailed studies (as envisaged by Policy Initiative 3). On the basis of the plot density figures used above (15 homes for at least 45 persons per acre) we can also estimate the number of homes that could be provided and the number of people housed in these areas.

## Table 4 Estimate of Surplus Land and Potential for Homes in Metropolitan County Areas

| Area | No. of Boroughs | Land possibly available (acres) | Possible no. of: Homes | /Peoplehoused |
|---|---|---|---|---|
| Greater Manchester | 10 | 250 | 3750 | 11250 |
| Merseyside | 5 | 125 | 1875 | 5625 |
| South Yorkshire | 4 | 100 | 1500 | 4500 |
| Tyne and Wear | 5 | 125 | 1875 | 5625 |
| West Midlands | 7 | 175 | 2625 | 7875 |
| West Yorkshire | 5 | 125 | 1875 | 5625 |

All this land should be made available for housing by local authorities *free of charge*. This is possible *now* within current law: a council may decide to use its own land for homes just as it decides to use land for schools, offices and roads. All it takes is the political will.

## 2. Costs

The provision of homes on such a large scale will need a considerable amount of money, even if costs per unit are kept as low as possible. The CHISEL costings used in Chapter 4 showed that a bed space can be provided for approximately £10,000 (excluding the cost of the land). On the basis of this figure, the cost of providing homes for 13,500 people in London would be £135,000,000. However, larger self-build schemes could benefit from economies of scale, as demonstrated by a highly-detailed document drawn up by CHISEL and Architype, *Self-Build Housing - Volume Bid*.[1] The projection of costs in this bid 'is based on assumptions made after careful consideration and research into current costs and discussion amongst participants with respect to the economics of scale which could be achieved.'[2] The conclusions were that big savings could be made on large-scale schemes: 40% on groundwork; 20% on materials; 13% on site management; 55% on architectural fees; and 48% on development allowances, as well as corresponding percentage reductions on other 'on-costs' such as legal fees and training. The total cost of the Volume Bid scheme, excluding the land element, was estimated at £11,230,675. This would provide housing for 1,320 people (see Tables 5 and 6) and reduce the cost of each bed space to £8,508.

**Table 5  Volume Self-Build - Details of accommodation provided**

| House type | Occupants | Bedrooms | Habitable rooms | Number of units | Total habitable rooms | Total no.of people housed |
|---|---|---|---|---|---|---|
| A | 2 | 1 | 2 | 100 | 200 | 200 |
| B | 3 | 2 | 3 | 200 | 600 | 600 |
| C | 5 | 3 | 4 | 80 | 320 | 400 |
| D | 6 | 4 | 5 | 20 | 100 | 120 |
| Totals | | | | 400 | 1220 | 1320 |

**Table 6  Analysis of housing provision**

| House type | Housing for the homeless | Black and ethnic minorities | Disabled | Foyer i.e. people from short-life houses | Total units |
|---|---|---|---|---|---|
| A | | 30 | 20 | 50 | 100 |
| B | 100 | 50 | 25 | 25 | 200 |
| C | 50 | 30 | | | 80 |
| D | 10 | 10 | | | 20 |
| Total | 160 | 120 | 45 | 75 | 400 |

On the basis of these calculations, the total cost of providing 13,500 bed spaces in London would be £114,750,000 (13,500 x £8,500 per bed space). However, we could reasonably assume *even greater* savings in view of the larger scale of operation we are proposing—perhaps to around £8,000 per bed space. The overall cost of housing 13,500 homeless people at £8,000 per bed space would be £108,000,000.

We were keen to discover just how much costs could be reduced, so we commissioned Architype to design and estimate the costs of basic, self-build, emergency accommodation. Their full report is reproduced as Appendix 1 to this Chapter. For this very basic design, we can see that the cost of a 2-bedroomed, 3-bed space bungalow unit is £10,100 (£3,366 per bed space); that of a 3-bedroomed, 4-bed space unit is £12,200 (£3,050 per bed space); and that of a 4-bedroomed, 6-bed space unit is £13,700 (£2,283 per bed space). These figures include site costs, such as the installation of main services, but exclude VAT (which is recoverable anyway) and consultants fees and supervision costs. In our calculations we also exclude these costs because, spread over a large number of units, they would add an insignificant amount to the cost of each unit and, as a matter of policy, a Green local authority would make existing council staff available to fulfill these roles.

The figures in the Appendix also exclude the cost of access roads, footpaths and fencing, for the reasons stated by Architype. We also exclude the cost of these from our calculations because we have allowed for no economies of scale in our estimates and because we have assumed an average cost per bed space which is on the high side. These two factors will, we believe, offset any extra costs that have been excluded. Therefore, we assume an average cost per bed space of £3,000. The cost of providing 13,500 bed spaces on the 300 acres of land available in London could thus be reduced to £40,500,000.

These figures compare favourably with yet another highly original Architype scheme for the Diggers Self-Build Housing Co-operative in Brighton. In this scheme, the concept of short-life, relocatable self-build was developed. The scheme provided small two- and three- bedroomed bungalows for four and six people respectively and, at 1987 prices, cost an average of £2,700 per bed space.[3] Assuming an increase in costs since 1987, we conclude that the cost of building these units would now be slightly more than the £3,000 average cost per bed space of the basic, emergency units designed for us by Architype.

The Diggers scheme does have one great advantage—the units are relocatable. This makes large-scale, self-build schemes on Part X land even more viable because the houses can be moved should the local authority wish to use the land at some time in the future. Relocatable housing also means that vacant land not owned by the local housing authority may also be usable for a number of years without jeopardising any long-term plans the owner might have. This could apply particularly well to land being acquired by county councils or the Department of Transport in advance of future road schemes. Even private developers may be amenable to releasing land for five to ten years in the knowledge that they can be sure of getting it back when they need it. The specialist body which deals with short-life houses, the Empty Homes Agency, might well consider it worthwhile to promote and secure the use of 'short-life land'. The fact that the accommodation provided in this way is short-life has implications on the funding of these schemes (see below).

There are, therefore, five possible costings for 13,500 bed spaces for homeless people in London:

Basic CHISEL costs
    (@ £10,000 per bed space)      £135,000,000

Volume Self-Build costs
    (@ £8,500 per bed space)      £114,750,000

Volume Self-Build costs + extra savings
    (@ £8,000 per bed space)      £108,000,000

Architype emergency unit costs
    (@ £3,000 per bed space)      £40,500,000

Diggers Relocatable Self-Build
    (@ £3,000+ per bed space)      £40,500,000+

Where could this money come from if there was no help from central government? We list a number of alternatives below.

## Funding - Method 1: Redirecting Bed and Breakfast

We proposed this method of funding in Policy Initiative 5 in Chapter 4. We showed that, in London, the average cost of bed and breakfast is £270 per week whereas an 'in lieu of bed and breakfast' unit is cheaper, costing £100 per week per family, and we estimated that, if 3,000 'in lieu of bed and breakfast' units were provided, at least £20,000,000 could be saved on bed and breakfast bills in one year. This money could be used by local authorities to fund an all-London, cross-borough, large-scale, self-build policy.

There are various ways in which this money can be saved and redirected into self-build schemes. All involve local authorities drawing up their annual bed and breakfast budgets in exactly the same way they do every year, on the basis of the average cost of £270 per week per family. There are then three possible ways of proceeding. The advantage of all of them is that no change in legislation is required as housing authorities already have a discretionary power to provide accommodation for the so-called non-priority classes of homeless people.

(a) Each council individually approaches the emergency housing teams set up to provide 'in lieu of bed and breakfast' accommodation. They discuss the number of units that the council are likely to want along with the number of units that look likely to be provided in the course of the financial year. The local authority can then estimate the *savings* it can make on its bed and breakfast bill as a result of this cheaper provision. For example, a council estimates that it will receive a total of 1,000 unit-weeks of accommodation 'in lieu of bed and breakfast'; for each unit-week it pays £100 and saves £170, thereby saving a grand total of £170,000 over the 1,000 unit-weeks. This money can be made available at once to fund the self-build schemes described above.

(b) Each council makes an arrangement with one of the agencies providing 'in lieu of bed and breakfast' units. The council pays the agency the bed and breakfast rate of £270 per week although it only costs the agency £100 per week to provide the unit. The agency therefore makes a weekly 'profit' of £170 on each unit. The agency calculates its annual 'profits' and makes this sum available to fund self-build schemes.

Note: in both a) and b) the council 'spends' the same amount of money: in a) it spends £100 per week on an 'in lieu of bed and breakfast' unit, saves £170 and spends that on self-build schemes; in b) it spends all £270 on an 'in lieu of bed and breakfast' unit and it is the agency who puts the 'profit' of £170 towards self-build schemes.

(c) An all-London Emergency Housing Committee (EHC) is set up consisting, perhaps, of representives from the providing agencies and nominees from the boroughs. The EHC approaches the boroughs to seek *advance* payments for the use of 'in lieu of bed and breakfast' units for (say) six months and obtains an immediate surplus for investing in self-build schemes.

This method may be the best way of proceeding as it will enable a cross-borough housing pool to be utilised (see Policy Initiative 6) and it will lessen parochialism regarding funding of self-build schemes. It is essential that schemes are funded according to need and the ability to proceed, rather than on the basis of which homeless people come from which borough. London's homeless are London's homeless: they do not belong to any one borough and borough boundaries should play no part in provision under this emergency scheme.

The Emergency Housing Committee is suggested as advice to enable schemes to proceed: we have no wish to establish a centralised bureaucracy. If better ways of proceeding can be found then they should be set up. It is the principle and the policy that is important, not the mechanism. We have shown that such a scheme can work and a Green council will have the political will to take the decisions required to implement it. Will the other political parties do likewise?

Outside London the same principle can be applied. In Chapter 4, we compared the average bed and breakfast cost of £165 per week with the estimated cost of £66 per week for an 'in lieu of bed and breakfast' unit—an average weekly saving of £100 per unit. Once an 'in lieu of bed and breakfast' scheme is operating, the estimated savings can be redirected to self-build schemes at no extra cost to the local authority. The opportunities for cross-council co-operation may be much less, or even non-existent, in some areas but this does not present any great hurdle: putting the savings of £100 per week per unit into self-build housing can easily be implemented by any local authority acting alone (as in (a) above).

An authority could also apply the same principle to the private leasing schemes we mentioned in Chapter 4: they could estimate their annual bed and breakfast budget and any money saved through private leasing arrangements could be put towards this emergency programme.

Even in areas where only small savings can be made, this process is worthwhile: £27,000 saved would enable two units for 12 single homeless people to be built. It would be an important start; it would be a sign of hope to the homeless and show them that the political will is there to help them.

### Funding - Method 2: Local Authority Loans

A second method of financing this crash programme could be through loans from the local authority. This could work as follows:

Let us take the cheapest possible option that we have suggested: the 4-bedroomed, 6-bed space, emergency unit designed for us by Architype, costing £2,283 per bed space. If a local authority loaned this money to a self-build group on an interest-free basis, the loan repayments over one year would be £43.90 per person per week; a loan over two years would entail weekly payments of £21.95 per person. The rents of the CHISEL self-build schemes were £38.00 per week but this

70

amount also covered other elements—for example, training, repairs and management (see Policy Initiative 11, Chapter 4). Thus, although a rent of £43.90 per week would still constitute a cheap and affordable rent, it would only cover the loan repayments and leave no money to cover the other costs.

There are two solutions to this problem: firstly, the council could allow repayments over a longer period of two or three years. This would be the ideal solution as it would reduce the loan repayment element in the rent leaving the remainder free to cover other costs. However, we can foresee difficulties with this: the council's auditor might comment on an increase in loan debt in the council's annual accounts and the tying-up of capital for two or three years would adversely affect other services the council provided.

It is the second solution, therefore which seems more practicable: a one-year loan with *all* of the rent in the first year going towards repayments. This means that the council would carry little or no debt into the following year's accounts; also, money that the council had budgetted to spend at the *end* of the financial year could be used for the loans and then still spent as planned because all or most of the loan will have been repaid by that time.

What about the other elements in the CHISEL rent—management and repairs, for instance? In the first year there should be few repairs, but where they do occur they can be carried out by the self-builders. Materials could be provided by a local housing association with the co-operative contracting to pay for them in the *next* financial year, when the loan repayment element in the rent would be nil. Similarly with management and training charges: the self-builders would buy them in the first year and pay for them in the second year when all their loans had been repaid. If necessary, the council could underwrite these arrangements to give all the providers of these services more security.

We believe that this can work although we accept it is not ideal. It will require commitment and goodwill—but it is *just* possible. We are proposing arrangements such as these in order to get round government inertia and spending regulations. Until the government adopt sensible funding measures, a Green council will look for ways that will enable it to start a major self-build programme.

## Funding - Method 3: Secured Loans

Yet another method of funding the scheme could be by means of loans from building societies or other commercial agencies. A self-help group could approach a society for a small loan of, say, £2,500 per bed space to be repaid over five or ten years. The repayments, even allowing for interest, would be small because of the much longer repayment period and thus could be paid out of a normal rental charge. But would a loan be forthcoming? At first, there would be very considerable reluctance by building societies to give loans to these schemes because of lack of security: there would be no house, only a site and a plan. There are two ways of overcoming this hurdle: the council could *guarantee* the loan for the critical period while the house was being built (and this could be *as little as three weeks*—see below). When it was finished, the self-build group could apply to a building society for a mortgage using the house as security *or* the council could provide a bridging loan for the building period, at the end of which the self-build group could obtain a building society mortgage and use it to repay the bridging loan. Either way, finance need not be a hindrance to the success of these schemes.

## Funding - Method 4: Mini-HAG

We mentioned Housing Association Grants (HAG) in Chapter 4. Mini-Housing Association Grant (Mini-HAG) are grants payable by the Housing Corporation on *short-life* housing—that is, units provided for up to 10 years. Thus, the Diggers relocatable houses would qualify for mini-HAG. This source of funds has been increasing and we believe it could provide another useful method of funding for our crash programme.

## Environmental Considerations

We would ensure, as far as possible, that all units of 'in lieu of bed and breakfast' accommodation have basic thermal insulation. As we stressed in Chapter 3, this is important for the environment, as it reduces energy wastage and pollution, and for the people living in the property, as it reduces fuel bills. Keeping a short-life house warm is sometimes difficult and can result in debt and disconnections. A few pounds spent on basic insulation measures can make even temporary accommodation comfortable at reasonable cost.

For the self-build schemes, which will provide homes for much longer periods, environmental considerations are just as essential. It is important, therefore, that all the schemes we have discussed do provide, to varying degrees, environmentally-friendly housing. The Volume Self-Build scheme, for instance, is 'based on ecological principles which aim to limit energy use and pollution...for the self-builders the major advantages are significantly lower running costs and healthier homes to live in.'[4] In particular, the Volume Self-Build scheme achieves:

- a National Home Energy Rating (NHER) of between 9 out of 10 and 10 out of 10; indeed, some existing units designed by Architype achieve *annual* space-heating costs of only £30[5]
- use of insulation made from recycled newspaper
- energy efficient boilers
- use of softwood, a renewable low-energy resource
- utilisation of passive solar gain and natural ventilation
- use of British-grown rather than imported timber where possible.[6]

We also asked Architype to bear environmental considerations in mind when designing the cheaper, emergency units—with the result that the thermal insulation of this accommodation (provided at rock-bottom costs) will be 'at least to current building regulation standard and possibly better.'[7] We would like to see NHER standards raised above the current inadequate rating of 7, and we believe that the scale of our proposed operation would enable us to develop an equally cheap model unit with a higher NHER rating. The Volume Self-Build scheme shows that very considerable economies of scale can be made. This money could then be put towards achieving NHER standards of 8 or 9, thus making our emergency units even more environmentally-friendly and cheaper to heat.

The issue of energy conservation should be discussed with the homeless: those local authorities[8] that have involved tenants in energy conservation schemes have reported that the very act of talking to the occupiers has increased their awareness and enthusiasm for energy efficency measures. The processes involved in a successful scheme are political and educational, as well as technical.

In the final analysis, however, we believe that energy conservation, like homelessness, is a national issue requiring action and resources by central government. This crash programme is but an important start.

## How

Our programme is based on mutual aid principles: the effort and commitment of the homeless and the experience and expertise of the specialist agencies (such as CHISEL and Architype) combined with the promotional and enabling role of local authorities.

This will not happen without extra efforts by local councils. A Green local authority will reach out to the homeless: to squatters; to cardboard city dwellers; to the childless couples with no hope of securing accommodation; to families in bed and breakfast; to women in refuges; to black and other ethnic groups; and to homeless persons with disabilities. All these people can participate in self-build schemes. There is, for example, a self-build scheme currently being operated by disabled people in Colchester, Essex.

We will involve homeless people in our empty property and vacant land strategies by offering them an active role in this programme; we will invite them to form themselves into self-build housing co-operatives;[9] and we will employ or redeploy council staff to provide the necessary advice and back up.

We will organise the necessary training for the many hundreds of self-help groups that will come into existence, using the detailed training programme in self-build, site organisation and the organisation of housing co-operatives which has already been developed by CHISEL and Architype.[10] We will also enable and encourage trainees from Training and Enterprise Councils and other agencies to become involved;[11] and we will request and encourage organisations such as the Empty Homes Agency to help with this initiative.

We will make available the plots of land suitable for housing from the Part X registers; we will use council resources to facilitate the drawing-up of plans for self-build projects by groups of homeless people;[12] and finally, we will make available all moneys saved on bed and breakfast bills to finance the materials and other costs of this extensive self-build programme.

We have no doubt that the response from homeless people will be massive. Already, tens of thousands of homeless people spend much of their own time and money repairing derelict and run-down houses when they squat in them; already, there are waiting lists for the limited funds available for self-build schemes; the enormous success of the 'legal squatting' movement, begun in Lewisham in 1969, shows that homeless and badly-housed people respond enthusiastically when they are offered the opportunity to participate in the creation of better accommodation. Few councils recognize the creative ability of homeless people. A notable exception is Mansfield District Council who, in conjunction with Nottingham Community Housing Association and GAP UK (Guaranteed Accommodation

Project - a specialist consultancy) has brought together empty private houses, the unemployed and the homeless. The Council has acquired run-down empty houses and, with GAP and the Training Enterprise Council, organised work training on the properties for groups of unemployed and homeless people. The 'self-helpers' learn new trades and eventually live in the homes they have refurbished. It is both a housing and a training scheme with a difference–it involves people. Whole families attend organisation meetings and central direction is at a minimum ('the best management is no management'). It is the most exciting mutual aid scheme we have seen. A Green council will develop this example and offer the homeless advice, support, training and accommodation—rather than abuse, hostility and rejection.

The start date for this operation is *now*, so that within months, rather than years, the use of bed and breakfast can be drastically reduced and the single homeless and other non-priority classes can move onto sites to start building their own homes. We asked our consultants, Architype, for an assessment of the time it might take to build the emergency units that they designed for us. They said: 'The answer must lie in the range between 3 weeks for a small, well-organised team of 3 or 4 working long hours on a 2-bedroomed bungalow to 60 weeks for a single person of moderate skill working part time to build a 3-bedroom house.' They also reported that 'a team of 20 people would be good for a development of 20 houses.' [13] The ideal of twenty people working on twenty houses may not be possible to achieve on every site and, as our schemes are based on *mutual* aid, we do not envisage one person being left alone for sixty weeks to build a house. Thus, the average construction time might run into months rather than weeks, with some units being ready very quickly after the commencement of works and others taking longer.

The most exciting prospect is that these schemes, if adopted immediately, could start to produce homes before the cold of next winter sets in. This would mean that some homeless people, at least, would have a warm place to live that they could call their own home.

Self-build schemes do not only build houses: 'Self-building is without a doubt one of the most effective ways of consolidating a self-sustaining community...self-builders will be able to learn and develop a range of new skills...and this will help individual members to fulfill a more effective role in society and improve their prospects...but the main benefit will be to help end the dependancy of the homeless and inadequately housed who benefit from it, on forms of provision and management that disempower them...they reaffirm their role as pivotal participants in the housing process, rather than its passive beneficiaries.'[14] This programme could give back the self-respect that months and years of sleeping rough and being forced into bed and breakfast can so easily undermine. It is a programme for hope as well as homes—a Green programme of self-help and mutual aid—a programme that can work.

## Footnotes

1. *Self-Build Housing - Volume Bid,,* CHISEL and Architype, June 1993
2. ibid. p.10
3. *Relocatable Self-Build Houses,* Architype Design Co-operative (for Diggers Self-Build Housing Co-operative)
4. *Volume Bid* op. cit. p.17
5. ibid. p.18
6. ibid. pp.17-18
7. See Appendix 1 to this Chapter
8. For example, Newark and Sherwood District Council
9. *Self-Build Housing Co-operatives: Rental,* Charlie Cattel, Industrial Common Ownership Movement
10. *Volume Bid* op. cit.
11. *Volume Bid* op. cit.; also the GAP scheme run by Mansfield District Council
12. See, for example, *The Self-Build Book* by Jon Broome and Brian Richardson, Green Books, 1991
13. See Appendix 1 to this Chapter
14. *Volume Bid* op. cit. p.29

## APPENDIX 1

Report of Architype Design Co-operative to Ron Bailey, Green Party Campaigns Organiser, 13th December 1993.

### Self-Build for Single Homeless

[i] Drawings 1500/04 to 06 show 2, 3 and 4 bedroom bungalows. The layout of these is intended to offer as much privacy within the dwelling as possible. In this way each individual bedroom occupies its own wing of the building. This adds a certain amount of area and therefore cost. There is only a single living space in these plans which assumes that the residents are either in the communal kitchen/dining room or in their own private bedroom.

[ii] I estimate that self-build costs would be:
    2 bedroom bungalow — £10,000
    3 bedroom bungalow — £12,200
    4 bedroom bungalow — £13,700

[iii] Difficult to estimate the time to self-build because it depends on many variables including how many people, how much time per week and what level of skill? The answer must lie in the range between 3 weeks for a small, well-organised team of 3 or 4 working long hours on a two-bedroom bungalow to 60 weeks for a single person of moderate skill working part-time to build a 3-bedroom house.

[iv] A team of 20 people would be good for a development of 20 houses.

[v] The energy efficiency of these dwellings would be relatively good, i.e. at least to current Building Regulations standard and probably better.

The costs quoted:
- include £1700 per dwelling for mains services for a
    self-built house, made up as follows -
    £1500 water, £200 electricity
- assume normal foundation conditions - extra cost
    would be incurred for special foundations
- exclude site development costs for roads, fencing and
    footpaths as these are completely dependent on
    the particular site
- exclude fees as these are very dependent on numbers
- exclude the cost of any site supervisor that may be required
    for self-build options
- exclude VAT as this should be recoverable if rated as new
    housing.

Jon Broome,
for Architype.

# Architype Emergency Units - Sketch Drawing 1500/04
## (two-bedroom unit)

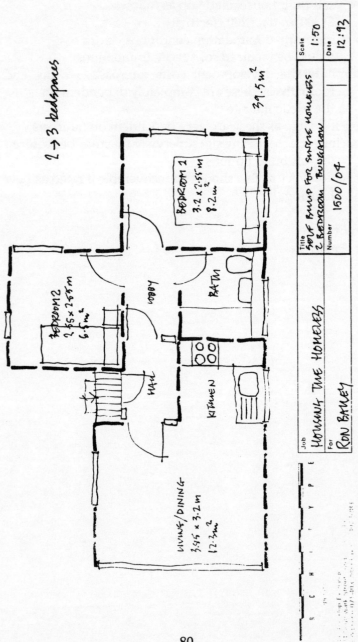

2 → 3 bedspaces

39.5 m²

BEDROOM 1
3.2 x 2.55 m
8.2 m²

BATH

BEDROOM 2
2.55 x 2.65 m
6.5 m²

1.800

KITCHEN

HALL

LIVING / DINING
3.45 x 3.2 m
12.3 m²

| Job | | Scale |
|---|---|---|
| HOUSING THE HOMELESS | | 1:50 |
| Title SELF BUILD FOR SINGLE HOMELESS 2 BEDROOM THURSTON | | Date 12.93 |
| For RON BAILEY | Number 1500/04 | |

# Architype Emergency Units - Sketch Drawing 1500/05
## (three-bedroom unit)

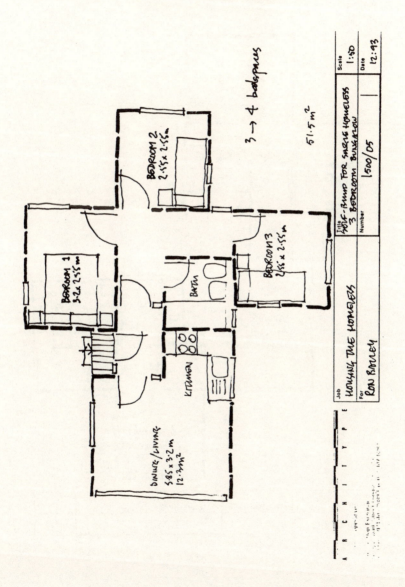

## Architype Emergency Units - Sketch Drawing 1500/06
## (four-bedroom unit)

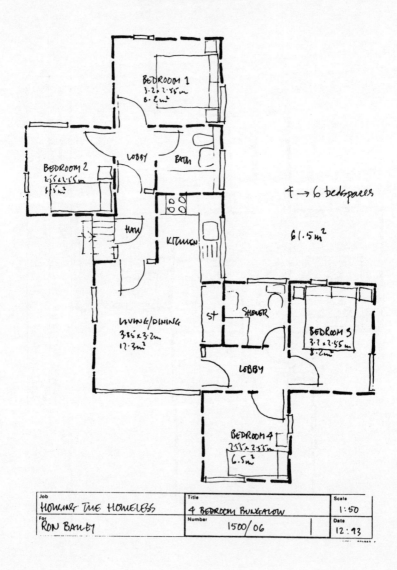

# 6 Homeless Persons and Mutual Aid Bill (Policy Initiative 16)

This Bill will introduce into Parliament an all-embracing new law to deal with homelessness and empty property. The basis of the Homeless Persons and Mutual Aid Bill is an amended and updated form of the Empty Property and Community Aid Bill which was supported by Shelter and introduced into the House of Commons in 1987 by Ken Hargreaves, then the Conservative M.P. for Hyndburn. We propose to introduce the new Bill into Parliament at the earliest opportunity. The full text of the Bill is printed in Appendix 1 to this Chapter. Its underlying approach accords with the philosophy we explained in Chapter 3 and its provisions bring together many of the Policy Initiatives proposed in this book.

**Part 1** deals with empty property strategies:

- Section 1 enacts Policy Initiative 2 by requiring councils to find out what empty properties are in their area and prepare strategies for bringing them back into use.
- Section 2 requires proper records to be kept of property in the council's ownership or in the ownership of other public bodies (listed in Schedule 1) that is empty for more than six months; the reasons for this; and also any proposals for use.
  Under Section 2(2) the Secretary of State may extend the list of public bodies in Schedule 1.
  Section 2(3) requires a list to be kept of properties upon which Empty Property Use Order action has been taken (see below) and it also gives councils a discretionary power to keep a register of all empty property.

**Part 2** gives councils the power to put Empty Property Use Orders (EPUOs) on property not in their ownership:

- In Section 3 a detailed procedure is laid down and safeguards built in. EPUO action is only possible if the property in question has been empty for more than a year. Before any action can be taken, the owner must be served with a notice giving him/her 21 days to either submit proposals for use or to notify the authority of his/her intention to do so within a reasonable period of time. There are also provisions for owners to seek exemption from the whole procedure.

- Section 4 finally gives the local authority the power to make an EPUO on any houses upon which notices have been served under Section 3 and in respect of which *no* proposals for use have been received, or where proposals have been received but not acted upon within a reasonable period of time and in respect of which no exemption has been sought or granted. Once an EPUO has been made the council must take immediate steps to bring the house back into use.

The Bill enables councils to use the EPUO'd houses themselves or hand them over to housing associations or self-help groups of homeless people. Thus, houses that the council cannot afford to repair can be taken over and used by such groups. The Bill also contains provisions enabling the council to obtain vacant possession at the end of the EPUO period so that the property can be handed back to the owner.

- Section 5 enables local people or parish councils to petition for an EPUO to be put on a property and a mechanism is laid down for this. The concept of citizen action is thus introduced into the procedure.

**Part 3** deals with mutual aid and self-help in more detail:

- Section 6 ensures that the empty property registers kept by councils are made open to inspection by housing associations and recognised voluntary bodies.

- Section 7 is the most important section: it gives real power
to housing associations, community groups and groups
of people in housing need (for example, single homeless
people, families in bed and breakfast, etc.). Where these
groups discover empty houses owned by local authorities
they can submit proposals requiring the Council to allow
them to use the properties. The Council must comply
unless they can show good reason for not doing so. The
onus is therefore on the council to give reasons for refusal.
This enacts Policy Initiative 7 in Chapter 4. Councils are
also required to inform people of their rights and to give
advice and assistance to groups of homeless people who
wish to submit proposals for use of empty houses. In this
way, the energy and abilities of homeless people can be
harnessed to deal with the disgrace of empty property, as
envisaged by Policy Initiative 8 in Chapter 4.

Section 7(4) specifically permits councils to guarantee
loans to homeless people made by Building Societies and
other bodies to enable them to repair empty properties.
The loans can then be repaid by the occupants as if they
were the 'rent' or 'mortgage' repayments. This will assist
in attracting funds to repair empty homes.

If enacted the Bill will provide a full statutory framework
for dealing with empty property to the best advantage of
homeless people. The Green Party will campaign vigorously
on an all-party basis for the enactment of this measure.

**APPENDIX Empty Property And Mutual Aid Bill**

**Part 1 Strategy for use of empty residential property**

1. (1) It shall be the duty of every local housing authority to
cause an inspection of their district to be made from
time to time with a view to ascertaining whether any
residential property is empty and to keep records of
all such inspections.

(2)   It shall be the duty of every local housing authority to consider the housing needs of their district with respect to the use of empty residential property and for that purpose to review the information which has been brought to their notice either as a result of inspections and surveys carried out under sub-section (1) above, or otherwise, and as often as the occasion arises, or within three months after notice has been given to them by the Secretary of State, to prepare and submit to the Secretary of State proposals for the use of empty residential property.

(3)   A local housing authority shall provide annually to the Secretary of State a statement of its strategy for bringing into use any residential property which it holds or has acquired, and which has remained vacant for six months or longer, and any such strategy statement shall be available for inspection by any member of the public at the offices of the authority at all reasonable hours, and any member of the public may make a copy of any such strategy on payment of a reasonable fee.

2. (1)   It shall be the duty of a local housing authority to maintain a register of all residential property in its ownership which has been empty for six months or longer, and such a register shall state the reasons that the property has been left empty and any proposals for its use, occupancy, letting or disposal.

(2)   Sub-section (1) above shall apply to empty property owned by any body listed in Schedule 1 to this Act and the Secretary of State may by Order add to that Schedule.

(3)   It shall be the duty of a local housing authority to maintain an up-to-date register of all properties upon which action is being or has been taken under Part 2 of this Act, and to take any other steps as the authority deems appropriate to keep a register of empty residential property not in its ownership.

## Part 2 Empty Property Use Orders

3. (1) Where a local housing authority is satisfied that:
   (a) any house, or self-contained separate flat within a house, which is empty, or
   (b) any building which contains residential accommodation comprising one or more separate dwellings which is empty

   and has remained empty for a period of at least twelve months they may serve on the owner of the house or building a notice requiring him to submit proposals for bringing the house or building into residential use.

   (2) A person upon whom a notice is served under sub-section (1) above shall within 21 days either submit to the authority proposals to bring the property into residential use, or notify the authority of his intention to do so within a reasonable period of time.

   (3) A person need not submit proposals under sub-section (2) above if he seeks exemption for one of the reasons listed in Schedule 2 of this Act and if such reason is accepted by the authority.

4. (1) A local housing authority may make an order under this section (in this Act called an Empty Property Use Order) with regard to any empty residential accommodation within their district if the person or persons having control of that accommodation have failed to provide satisfactory proposals for the use thereof or have failed to implement such proposals once agreed following the service of notice under Section 3 of this Act.

   (2) An Empty Property Use Order shall come into force as soon as it is made and as soon as is practicable after making the order the authority shall enter on the premises and take all such steps as appear to them to be required to enable the premises to be rendered capable of providing accommodation.

(3) Once an authority has taken steps under sub-section (2) above to render any properties capable of use then the authority shall use the premises as residential accommodation and paragraph 6 of Schedule 1 of the Housing Act 1985 shall apply to any tenancy granted persuant to this sub-section.

(4) A local housing authority may discharge its functions under sub-sections (2) and (3) above by making arrangements with a housing association or other voluntary body concerned with the provision of housing accommodation.

(5) An Empty Property Use Order shall last for a period not exceeding 5 years at the end of which time either

   (a) the authority may, with the consent of the owner, extend the Order for a further period of up to 5 years, or

   (b) the authority may issue a Compulsory Purchase Order on the property, or

   (c) the property shall revert to the owner or to any successor in title to the owner.

5. (1) The proper officer of the local housing authority shall make a report in writing to the authority whenever he is of the opinion

   (a) that a notice should be served under Section 3 of this Act

   (b) that an Order should be made under Section 4 of this Act

   and the authority shall take into consideration as soon as may be any such report made to them.

(2) If a complaint in writing is made that a notice should be served under Section 3 of this Act or an order made under Section 4 of this Act, to the proper office of the local housing authority by

   (a) a justice of the peace having jurisdiction in any part of their district, or

   (b) a parish or community council for a parish or community within their district, or

(c)  any 50 local government electors for the area, the
the proper officer shall forthwith inspect the house
and make a report in writing to the authority stating
the facts of the case and whether in his opinion action
ought to be taken pursuant to Section 3 or 4 of this Act.

(3)  The absence of a complaint under sub-section (2) does
not excuse the proper officer of the authority from his
duties under sub-section (1).

## Part 3  Mutual aid

6.  Any register maintained by a local housing authority
pursuant to Section 2 above shall be open to inspection
free of charge at the offices of the Council at all
reasonable hours by any housing association or other
voluntary body concerned with the provision of
housing accommodation and any such housing
association or voluntary body may make a copy of
any register on payment of a reasonable fee.

7. (1)  Where a local housing authority is unable to make use
of any empty or potentially residential property which
it holds or has acquired including any property held
by the authority pursuant to Part 2 of this Act and
which has remained empty, or is likely to remain
empty, for more than six months, it shall be under a
duty to consider any proposals from a local housing
association or other voluntary body for the use of the
property as residential accommodation.

(2)  Any proposals made by a housing association or other
voluntary body under sub-section (1) above shall be
accepted by the local housing authority unless
(a) the proposals would obstruct the strategy published
by the authority under this Act for bringing empty
property into use
(b) in the opinion of the local housing authority such
proposals are not practicable.

(3) Where a group of persons deemed by the authority to be in housing need wish to make proposals for the use of empty residential property under this Part of this Act then the authority shall take reasonable steps to provide such a group with advice and assistance in formulating any such proposals and in giving effect to such proposals.

(4) Any such assistance as mentioned in sub-section (3) above shall include the power to guarantee any loan made to such groups by any person in order to carry out rehabilitation work to facilitate the use of empty residential property under this Part of this Act.

(5) A local housing authority shall take reasonable steps to inform persons in housing need, housing associations and other voluntary bodies concerned with the provision of housing accommodation of the provisions of this Part of this Act.

## SCHEDULE 1

**Bodies whose properties are covered by Section 2**
(i)     County Councils
(ii)    Housing Associations
(iii)   British Rail
(iv)    Development Corporations
(v)     Government Departments
(vi)    District and Regional Health Authorities

## SCHEDULE 2

**Exemptions under Part 2**
(i)     MOD and Home Office property inside the perimeter of classified bases and prisons
(ii)    properties likely to be demolished within 6 months
(iii)   any other categories of property so designated by the Secretary of State after consultation with local authority organisations.

# 7 Squatting

In view of current government proposals, no book on homelessness would be complete without a consideration of the issue of squatting. The government's new proposals are to allow the owner of squatted property 'to apply to a civil court for an interim possession order without the squatters being present' and then, once the order has been made, the squatters would be 'given 24 hours to gather their belongings and leave the premises after the order is granted. If they fail to do so they will be committing a criminal offence and will be liable to arrest.'[1]

We think these proposals are little short of astonishing. Consider exactly what they mean: squatters (or, to be accurate, suspected squatters) will be tried in their absence—not because they have failed to turn up, or absconded or cannot be found but as a built-in, formal part of the system of justice in this country. Next, a court order will be made against them (again, in their absence) giving them 24 hours to leave their dwelling place and if they fail to comply with such an order, against which they have deliberately been denied the right to offer any defence or mitigation, they will be declared criminals.

These new criminals will then be arrested by the police. They and their children will begin to see the police as part of a system that has denied them a home and then criminalised them in their absence. The long-term effects of the resentment this will cause are quite frightening. The concept of policing by consent will be gone: there will be a significant under-class in society that will be permanently anti-police. Little wonder, therefore, that the Police Federation have opposed[2] the criminalisation of squatting. No murderer; no rapist; no fraudster; no drug trafficker; in fact, no one else except the homeless will be treated in such a way by our system of justice!

There are two aspects of these proposals that give cause for very serious concern from a judicial point of view. The first we referred to above: these new criminals, taken to court but given no right to be present and argue their case, are, in fact, only suspected squatters. The suspicion of squatting, given in the evidence of *one* side (the complainant's) to a judge, is all that is required to make them criminals. Despite the fact that the law at present gives judges no discretion once the squatting is proved (that is, a judge *must* make an immediate eviction order[3]), in 1991, 2,458 applications to a County Court for orders to evict squatters were unsuccessful.[4] However, the current law does give the suspected squatters a right to attend and argue their case. The failure of nearly 2,500 applications for eviction of squatters means one of two things: either that, in nearly 2,500 cases, the judges accepted that the defendants were squatters but deliberately and manifestly broke the law and refused to make orders against them or that, in nearly 2,500 cases, there was enough doubt about the application for eviction itself to persuade the judge not to make an immediate possession order. Our view is that the first explanation would be absurd and that the real reasons for the judges' refusals to order immediate eviction were doubts about the case. If the government's new proposals become law, all those people who might have successfully argued their case before a judge will be denied the right to do so.

The second judicial cause for concern relates to arguments that have been put both to the High Court and the County Court on behalf of squatters in a small minority of cases. We refer here to the defence 'Wednesbury unreasonableness'. This defence stems from the ruling of the Master of the Rolls in the case of Associated Provincial Picture Houses v Wednesbury Corporation.[5] This ruling means that, in cases involving a complaint brought by a public body, a defendant who may have no defence on the merits of the case may argue that, despite this, the decision of the public body to seek a court order in the first place is manifestly and demonstrably unreasonable. This ruling applies to cases brought by public bodies only. In such a case, the court will *not* grant the order applied for, in spite of the fact that there is no actual defence. It is important to emphasize the level of proof required: the decision of the public body to bring the case must not simply be unreasonable in the everyday sense of that word, it must be so unreasonable that no reasonable person properly advised could ever come to such a decision.

This concept has recently been applied to squatting cases[6] and in some instances has been accepted.[7] Consider the meaning of such cases: the public body (usually a local authority) has applied to the court for an eviction order; the squatters, accepting that they have no defence, have argued that in all the circumstances of their particular case, the decision of the local authority to seek an eviction order was 'Wednesbury unreasonable'. The judges have listened and have accepted that there is merit in the squatters' argument. We suggest, therefore, that the details of the case must have been quite extraordinary to convince a judge even to consider the 'Wednesbury unreasonable' argument. This in itself demonstrates the appallingly desperate plight of the squatters concerned. If the government's new proposals become law, the squatters—alone of all people in society—will be denied the right to make this argument as they will not be present.

Theoretical legal concepts apart (and that is not to minimise their importance) what do we think of all this from a 'lay' and a housing viewpoint? We begin by asking: 'Who are the squatters?' Such a question is clearly relevant when deciding on a policy response to a current issue.

We began by noting the comments of the government in the recent Home Office Consultation paper.[8] In paragraph 62 of that paper, the government asserted that it 'does not accept the claim that...squatting...(results) from social deprivation. Squatters are generally there by their own choice, moved by no more than self-gratification or an unreadiness to respect other people's rights.' As further evidence of this, the Consultation Paper states, at Paragraph 9, that 'cases (of squatting) involving very young children were negligible.'

The facts are very different. About one third of squatting households contain children[9] and this has been the case for over five years.[10] Under Section 58 of the housing Act 1985, all such families are statutorily homeless and so entitled to be accommodated by local authorities. This would often be bed and breakfast. The fact that they are squatting actually saves ratepayers vast amounts of money. Many other squatters need psychiatric help: since 1990 more than 28,000 hospital beds have been lost and only 5,000 residential places provided. Thus, many ill people have drifted into sleeping rough and squatting.[11] In addition, currently 2,000 squatters are women escaping violent partners.[12] Even more squatters are homeless single people for whom there is no statutory provision at all and for whom council waiting lists are meaningless. About one in twenty squatters (2,500 people) are ex-owner occupiers, evicted as they were unable to meet mortgage repayments.[13] In conclusion, therefore, all the available evidence shows that squatters are homeless people in desperate housing need, often with other social problems such as mental illness or the need to escape violence and harrassment. These are the people that the government is attempting to make into criminals.

Squatters, then, are homeless people: young single people, childless couples, families, people who have suffered abuse and violence and so on. Like all sections of society, there are among them the 'deserving' and the 'undeserving', the social and the anti-social. Does this mean, however, that because some squatters behave anti-socially, squatters are generally anti-social? This question can be answered by drawing an analogy: some company directors steal and defraud but that does not mean that 'company directors are thieves and fraudsters'. Similarly, while some squatters behave anti-socially, that does not mean that 'squatters are anti-social'. Any anti-social behaviour by squatters should be dealt with under the laws which exist to deal with such behaviour. The problem is those people in the squatting community who behave badly *not* the nature of the tenure of the homes in which they live.

The crucial question is this: is squatting *per se* always and without exception anti-social? Even if the answer to that question is 'yes', is squatting anti-social enough to be subjected to the draconian measures proposed by the government? Is squatting simply theft of other people's houses? Are squatters therefore akin to thieves and other criminals? The government's new proposals are dependent upon such beliefs being correct but we challenge them on the basis of historical and current evidence.

The current squatting movement started on 1st December 1968, with a token four-hour occupation of a block of luxury flats which had been empty for years. The 'crunch' came on 9th February 1969 when a number of homeless families and their supporters occupied houses owned by the London Borough of Redbridge. These houses had been acquired by the council in advance of a proposed town centre redevelopment plan due to start in two phases in 1973 and 1977. The houses had many years life before possible demolition: they were in good condition and on a number of occasions the council itself had passed resolutions to carry out repairs and utilise them. These resolutions had been defied by the (then) chair of the council's Town Centre Redevelopment Committee who had ordered that the houses be boarded up.[14]

At that time, there were large numbers of homeless families living in appalling conditions in homeless hostels[15] and there were thousands of children in care simply because their parents were homeless. This situation prompted local housing associations and Shelter to ask the council to use the homes or, at least, permit their use by officially-registered housing associations at no cost to the council. The council refused all such requests and the houses stayed boarded up. Local residents were worried about the houses remaining empty because of the resulting loss of rate revenue by the council and, more importantly, because the sight of increasing numbers of abandoned and boarded-up houses made the whole area look run-down. This situation affected the legal democratic rights of the residents. The council's redevelopment ideas were at that time (1969) only proposals: they were due to be argued out at a statutory public inquiry to be held in 1972. At that inquiry, the residents were planning to argue that the whole area was a highly desirable residential area and totally unsuitable for wholesale demolition and redevelopment—but how could they advance this argument when, in effect, the council was systematically rigging the evidence by boarding up houses and running the area down. The residents' case was being effectively destroyed by the council.

Against this background, the London Squatters Campaign assisted homeless families to move into the empty houses. Some of the families were from hostels and some had children in care. We ask: Whose property were those families stealing? Which housing list were they jumping? Who was it who was behaving anti-socially—the squatters occupying the derelict houses or the council which was wasting resources, deliberately running down the area in advance of the public inquiry and then, in response to the squatters, sending in teams of workmen to smash the homes to pieces by removing staircases and sawing through joists? To make sure the job was done thoroughly, the council also employed a private army of so-called 'professional bailiffs' who ran amok in the area smashing one pregnant woman in the stomach with iron bars, breaking another man's jaw and threatening to murder the author of this book.[16]

Some readers may decide: 'Yes, I can see things were bad but the squatters still shouldn't have done it'. In response to this, we make two further points. Firstly, we ask: 'What would you have done instead?' Everything else had been tried. Protests by Shelter and the residents had been ignored: there was no remaining alternative. Secondly, even if some people still cannot support the squatters, were their actions so anti-social as to warrant the draconian measures which the government now proposes—a court hearing *in their absence* and criminalisation *within 24 hours* of that hearing? Had the government's current proposals been law in 1969, this is what would have happened: the squatters would have been arrested and their children put back into care; the houses would have stood empty for 10 years; the area run down; and the residents' democratic right to argue their case at a public inquiry destroyed.

And perhaps, even more importantly, Councillor Herbert Eames, Chair of Lewisham Borough Council's Housing Committee, would not have been given the opportunity to take the courageous and visionary decisions which he was faced with a few months later.

In the autumn of 1969, after Redbridge Council had been brought to their knees by the squatters' campaign and the media publicity, the London Squatters turned their attention to the Conservative-controlled London Borough of Lewisham, where there were also large numbers of empty houses abandoned by the council. Two families were helped to squat in houses in Lee Green. Some Lewisham councillors wanted a Redbridge-style battle to remove the squatters but Herbert Eames, Conservative Chair of the Housing Committee, urged caution. He met the squatters and listened to them. The squatters argued that the houses were not going to be used; the families were in desperate housing need; the occupation would cost the council nothing as the squatters' organisation would carry out any necessary minor repairs; and the squatting group would agree to vacate the houses when they were genuinely needed by the council. Indeed, we pointed out to Councillor Eames, why stop at the two houses already squatted? There was a large number of empty council-owned homes in Lewisham with many years life before the council needed them: why not apply this principle to all of them?

Such a suggestion would be manifest common sense now: in 1969, in the wake of the massive battles in Redbridge and in the complete absence of any model on which to base it, the idea appeared to many to be beyond the pale. These anarchist squatters, fresh from fighting bloody battles with hired thugs in Redbridge, were asking Conservative Lewisham Council via its Housing Chairperson, and a solicitor at that, not only to sanction the initial squat of the two houses in Lee Green but also to hand over dozens of other empty homes.

If it was not quite revolution, it was certainly unheard of—but Herbert Eames listened. He could see the logic and common sense of the idea; he knew that the families were in desperate housing need. He also listened when the activists supporting the families explained that the anarchism which they espoused was not about chaos and social disorder but about mutual aid and personal and community responsibility. Councillor Eames thought it over and (metaphorically) coming from the other end of the world, had the courage and the vision to accept the sense and the value of it all. He therefore undertook to recommend the proposed arrangement to the Housing Committee of the Council.

He did not have an easy ride: some Conservative councillors opposed it. The Labour minority on the council were even more vehement in their opposition, accusing Eames of 'selling out to the anarchists' and calling for evictions. Finally, despite an initial vote against the scheme, Eames won by persuading the majority Conservative group on the council: many of them took the (reluctant) view that the risks of the deal were less than the risks of 'another Redbridge'. Thus, the Lewisham Family Squatting Association (LFSA) was born and for twenty-five years this organisation has been working with the council to ensure better use of empty property. Thousands of houses which would otherwise have stood empty have been brought into use and thousands of families helped. A letter from Herbert Eames tells of his feelings about the scheme and its successes (see opposite page).

The outcome would have been very different if the government's current proposals had then been in force. The squatters in Redbridge would have been criminals within a few weeks and could not have ventured into Lewisham to organise the two initial squats there. Even if another group, undeterred (unlikely) by the criminalisation of the Redbridge

London SE23
4th November 1970

Dear Ron Bailey,

Many thanks for your letter. I am sorry not to have been able to reply earlier, but I have been away for a few days.

Now that the Lewisham Borough Council has been co-operating with the Lewisham Family Squatting Association for almost a year, I think it is time to assess the position. I feel that the most important factor is that a very close understanding has been built up between the Council and your Association, and it is largely due to this close understanding that progress has been made, and there is now a feeling of trust between the Council officers and the officers of the Association.

The housing of over 90 families by the Association has shown that as a result of this close co-operation real results can be achieved. The Council was glad to find a use for houses which would otherwise have stood empty, as only those houses which the Council were not able to use itself have been made available to your Association...it has been very noticeable that the number of complaints about empty properties in the Borough have fallen very considerably in the last year...I am very grateful to your Association for the responsible attitude that it has adopted.

Yours sincerely,
(signed) Herbert Eames

Chairman, Housing Committee,
London Borough of Lewisham.

group, had organised the first squats in Lewisham, the idea could still not have happened, for two reasons: firstly, Eames lost an original vote in council and, although he won a few weeks later, by that time the council would have gone to court (without the squatters being present) and obtained an eviction order under which the squatters would have become criminals within twenty-four hours and so been arrested by the police. Many of the squatters, not wanting to risk this, would have just disappeared. Secondly, one of Eames' major selling points with the other councillors was the likelihood of 'another Redbridge' if there was no agreement between the Council and the squatters. The government's new proposals would have destroyed that particular argument and so this innovative scheme to use empty houses would never have happened.

The Lewisham arrangement has become the model for thousands of similar schemes in the years since 1969 and, as a result, tens of thousands (if not hundreds of thousands) of council-owned homes that would otherwise have stood empty have been occupied and hundreds of thousands of homeless people housed. This could not have happened if the government's current proposals had been law.

Even the Department of the Environment recognised the success of such arrangements. In a circular entitled 'Making the fullest use of all existing accommodation' issued in 1974 (nearly five years after the start of the Lewisham arrangement) the DoE states clearly at paragraph 9(i) that: 'housing authorities should be ready to work with local housing associations or voluntary bodies, *including reliable squatter organisations*' (our emphasis - RB). The Conservative Housing Minister at that time was Julian Amery M.P. The DoE could never have issued this exhortation—to ensure the best use of vacant dwellings—had the government's current proposals been law as there would have been no 'reliable squatter organisations'—only criminals.

We draw attention also to the words of the current Housing Minister's Special Adviser on empty property, Antony Fletcher. Fletcher has been involved in promoting the use of empty property since 1969 and is an experienced and reliable witness of events:

'The story of the birth and early life of the Lewisham Family Squatting Association—LFSA—is a model deserving to be copied by other public authorities all over the country. It is a shining example of effective co-operation developing from a situation of trespass and conflict and of many people housed who would have been homeless.

'The LFSA continues to this day, though working on a smaller scale. It is an impressive example of how a flexible Council can allow ordinary people in great housing need to solve their own problems by self-help and without any call upon public funds. The tragedy is that this has not been copied in countless similar situations all over the country.' [17]

Antony Fletcher could not have made the call for this arrangement to be 'copied in countless similar situations all over the country' if the government's current proposals had been law, as there would have been no such arrangements to copy.

We cannot find any evidence to show that things have changed since then. There are more homeless people now than then; there are still empty properties; and yet the government is suggesting that any group of homeless people who occupy and try to renovate vacant houses should be subjected to a court process in their absence and criminalised within twenty-four hours.

Let us be more specific. Is there any justification for enacting new laws and court procedures which will mean that a group of homeless people occupying Nos.96 and 98 King George Street, London SE10, or Tower House in Stepney, or the empty Ministry of Defence flats in Shillingford Street, Westminster (see Chapter 2), would be treated by the law in a way that would not even be inflicted on murderers, rapists, fraudsters, gangsters and the like? This is what the government's new proposals would do.

Some might say that squatters have changed—that in 1969 they were 'responsible' but now they are not. Such a claim is absurd: there is nothing that makes the homeless of 1994 any different to the homeless of 1969 and we reiterate our point that the people who made the highly-praised arrangement in Lewisham were the same people who had fought the bloody battles with the private armies in Redbridge. Were they wild irresponsible anarchists in Redbridge one day who suddenly became pillars of respectability a month or so later in Lewisham—or do squatters, like everybody else, respond to the way they are treated and act accordingly?

Home Secretary Michael Howard has also claimed that squatters jump the housing queue, to the detriment of those patiently waiting their turn. In response, we make the following points:

(i) Our evidence shows that very many squatters are 'priority need' homeless people and are entitled by law to immediate housing. In fact, by squatting in old houses and buildings, they have often jumped *out* of the housing queue and therefore saved hundreds of thousands of pounds of public money on bed and breakfast bills in the process.

(ii) Where squatters occupy houses intended for people on housing waiting lists, it is usually because councils refuse to co-operate with the squatters by not setting up schemes to help them. The London Borough of Southwark is a good example. After a year-long battle in 1970-71, Southwark Council was pressurised to enter into a Lewisham-type agreement[18] but municipal socialism prevailed in the end and co-operation with self-help housing schemes soon ceased. Homeless people therefore had no knowledge of which abandoned houses the council intended to use and which were going to be left empty for years. Inevitably, as a direct result of this lack of knowledge, squatters sometimes occupied houses which were due to be used to rehouse people from the housing waiting list. The solution to such a situation is far more simple than the proposed draconian measures to criminalise homelessness: the government should introduce measures to ensure full use of empty homes. It is significant that the problem did not arise in Lewisham and it could have been eradicated from Southwark (or certainly made insignificant) if the council had had the vision, courage and concern of Herbert Eames.

(iii) We know, however, that, in these days of hopelessness for the homeless, some squatters do occupy homes that the council wants to use, even in areas where the council co-operates with self-help schemes. Such actions have been criminal since the Criminal Law Act of 1978. There may be a case (although at present we doubt it) for the procedures under that Act to be amended or fine-tuned but any such amendment should be directed specifically at those squatters who occupy other people's homes or prospective homes and not at squatters who occupy homes that will be left empty.

Thus far, we have dealt with squatting in council-owned property—but what of private property? What of the oft-. quoted cases of people arriving back from holiday to find their homes occupied? There have been a handful of reported cases since squatting re-started in 1969. At first sight, the remarkable point is the small number of these cases but, on reflection, it is obvious why: squatters need and want to live in the houses they have occupied. Therefore, they seek *empty* homes, not places where they know they can expect trouble.

However, even a handful of these cases is too many. We accept that there may be other lesser wrongs committed by squatters, such as occupation of an empty private home where the owner is waiting to move in or where builders are due to start renovation work in the next week or so. In these cases, squatting can cause hardship to innocent private owners. What is the remedy in such exceptional circumstances?

We can also see that there may be a case (although we remain to be convinced of this) for speeding up procedures to enable wronged private owners to regain possession of their homes quickly and cheaply but such changes must be *specific to* this particular wrong rather than aimed at all squatters. Even in these exceptional cases, the implementation of the government's new measures must be viewed as totally unjustified and unjust.

Finally, should any new remedies be directed at all squatting in privately-owned property? We say 'no'. Take the the abandoned and derelict privately-owned houses described in Chapter 2: imagine that a group of homeless people, seeking shelter during a cold winter, occupied the 400 empty flats in Artillery Row near Victoria Station that have stood empty for 10 years; or another group decided to live in the empty house in Munster Square, owned and kept empty for six years by the Diocese of London; and suppose the squatters carried out major repairs and lived there peacably for some years and then the owners eventually arrived on the scene demanding that the squatters leave. Can it really be seriously suggested that it is fair and just to apply the government's new procedures to these people? We can see no justification for denying such squatters the right to a court hearing and making them criminals in their absence. For owners of such buildings, the current court remedies are adequate.

In conclusion, therefore, our policy on squatting and squatters, based on all the available evidence, is:

1. Squatters are homeless people and should be viewed as such. This is not an opinion; it is a fact.

2. Squatting in council-owned property has led to many important policy changes and new initiatives which have improved the use of housing stock and created homes for hundreds of thousands of people. This is not an opinion; it is a fact.

3. Had the government's current proposals been law those initiatives could never have happened. This is not an opinion; it is a fact.

4. Squatting has sometimes prevented councils from deliberately running areas down and denying residents their opportunity to argue their cases at public inquiries by 'rigging' the evidence. This is not an opinion; it is a fact.

5. Had the government's current proposals been law this unofficial method of protecting residents' democratic rights would not exist. This is not an opinion; it is a fact.

6. There are still too many empty publicly-owned

properties. This is not an opinion; it is a fact.

7. The homeless have not changed: they are still just the homeless, with the good and bad points of every other group in society. We see no evidence to the contrary.

8. Therefore, the government's proposals to introduce draconian new measures to criminalise all squatters are completely unjustified. This opinion is based upon a careful study of all the available evidence.

9. Where squatters occupy publicly-owned homes to the detriment of other intended occupiers, such actions are already a criminal offence. If new procedures were necessary we would not oppose them, providing they were specifically directed to deal with this wrong.

10. Similarly, with privately-owned empty homes: where innocent third parties suffer as a result of squatting, we believe that the current law, properly used, is sufficient to deal with this. However, if this were not the case, we would not oppose new powers provided they were specifically directed to deal with this particular wrong.

11. As regards a general, 'catch-all', new law relating to private homes, we reject this for the reasons stated.

12. Finally, we emphasise the two policies which we believe are crucial if squatters and other homeless people are to get fair and decent treatment:

(i) a national social housing scheme which would create jobs, homes and hope (in the medium term, at least); and

(ii) a crash emergency programme to deal with homelessness in the immediate and short term. This would involve the maximum use of all empty property by local authorities *in conjunction with the homeless*. Responsible public bodies should, as this book shows, work with the homeless — not fight them. It is mutual aid that is needed, not mutual hostility. It is Green Party politics and policies that will achieve this.

## Footnotes

1. *Faster Eviction for Squatters*, Press Briefing by Home Secretary Michael Howard MP, 4.11.93
2. Submission on the Home Office Consultation Paper on Squatting
3. High Court Order 113; County Court Order 26
4. Home Office Consultation Paper on Squatting, para.17
5. (1948) 1KB 223
6. West Glamorgan County Council v Rafferty and others
7. *Judicial Review as a Defence to Summary Possession Proceedings Against Squatters*, Sheelagh Robinson, Legal Action Bulletin, May 1989
8. Consultation Paper op.cit., para. 62
9. *A Crime to be Homeless?*, Squash, 1993
10. ibid.
11. ibid.
12. ibid.
13. ibid.
14. *Dictators in the Town Hall*, Ron Bailey, Housing Emergency Office, 1980
15. *Cathy Come Home*, Jeremy Sandford, 1965; *The Grief Report*, Ron Bailey and Joan Ruddock, Shelter, 1972
16. *The Squatters*, Ron Bailey Penguin, 1973; *Evicted*, London Squatters Campaign, 1969
17. *Homes Wasted*, Antony Fletcher, Shelter, 1982
18. *The Squatters* op.cit.